HORMONES HAIR ELASTICS AND HELMETS

THE ART AND SCIENCE OF SUCCESSFULLY COACHING FEMALE ATHLETES

Dr. Jeffrey R. LaCure, Psy.D, M.S.W., LICSW

TESTIMONIALS

"Dr. Jeff LaCure's book *Hormones, Hair Elastics, and Helmets* is the definitive resource in helping coaches understand and motivate female athletes at all levels. Dr. LaCure reminds us all that motivation through support and praise will bring success on and off the field of play. I thoroughly enjoyed this book and as an administrator I am reminded how important it is to support coaches and help parents understand that they need to allow their daughters to learn how to develop conflict-resolution skills."

—Tim Brillo, Head Girls Basketball Coach and Athletic Director
at Ludlow High School

"Dr. Jeff LaCure has written an amazingly comprehensive and eye-opening book on coaching female athletes. *Hormones, Hair Elastics, and Helmets* is a valuable addition to the coaching literature and is a needed resource for coaches, administrators, and parents. Coaches will be able to utilize the guidance provided by Dr. LaCure to build self-esteem, enhance performance, and develop strong team-chemistry. This is a must-read book that all coaches of female athletes, at any level, not only need to read, they need to incorporate Dr. LaCure's advice and suggestions into their daily practices and relationships with their athletes."

—Rita Atkinson, Head Women's Basketball Coach at Wheelock College

"Coach Jeff LaCure is always concerned about his players, on and off the field. He makes personal connections with everyone on the team to help us on the field, but also in our lives too. Coach LaCure motivates us to be the best players and teammates we can be."

—Megan Duquette and Brooke Bruneault, Co-Captains
for Ludlow High School Softball, 2017

"In *Hormones, Hair Elastics, and Helmets*, Dr. LaCure helps answer some of the questions those of us who coach women have been asking. He has provided us with a research-based guide to successfully coach female athletes. In a succinct, yet comprehensive manner, Dr. LaCure addresses everything from why female athletes join teams and play sports, to the physical and psychological differences between males and females, to gender-based differences in coaching women. This book will be a valuable and critical addition to the library of all coaches."

—Brian Wilson, Head Women's Basketball Coach at Connecticut College

"I have witnessed firsthand this new generation of female athletes growing up with unprecedented opportunities, far more than girls before them, and yet they seem to be consumed with issues of self-confidence, depression, and substance abuse. The athletic environment has provided a wonderful venue for all female athletes to find their voice and the relationships and connections they are so hungry to have. I can only hope the readers of *Hormones, Hair Elastics, and Helmets* will truly appreciate how young women can benefit from participation in athletics, but more importantly, what they can teach coaches from those experiences. Dr. LaCure has written an amazingly thoughtful, inspiring, and complete book that will help all coaches and athletic administrators rise to the challenge of being successful mentors and role-models for all female athletes."

—Dr. Andrew J. Pittington, Ph.D, Former Head Women's Basketball Coach
at Mount Ida College

To the loving memory of my father, Hilton George LaCure, Jr. and my son, Jeffrey Jr. You both have been my inspirational life coaches.

www.mascotbooks.com

Hormones, Hair Elastics, and Helmets:
The Art and Science of Successfully Coaching Female Athletes

For more information, please contact:
Mascot Books
620 Herndon Parkway #320
Herndon, VA 20170
info@mascotbooks.com

Library of Congress Control Number: 2017912777

CPSIA Code: PBANG1017A
ISBN: 978-1-62086-847-8

Printed in the United States

HORMONES HAIR ELASTICS AND HELMETS

THE ART AND SCIENCE OF
SUCCESSFULLY COACHING
FEMALE ATHLETES

Dr. Jeffrey R. LaCure, Psy.D, M.S.W., LICSW

TABLE OF CONTENTS

PART II
Coaching Male and Female Athletes:
The Similarities and the Differences
"Not Just One of the Boys"

PART VI

A Coaching Model Designed for Success

FOREWORD

As a first-year coach, or more accurately—basketball intern, at Williams College, I had the opportunity to simultaneously work under both the men's coach Dave Paulsen and the women's coach Pat Manning. As a newly minted college graduate I am sure that I did not appreciate the uniqueness of my situation, the chance to observe on an almost daily basis the distinct differences and similarities in coaching males and females. What I did know was that as much as I enjoyed coaching men, I felt most effective interacting with the women.

While coaching in my dual role, I noticed that one could be much more positive and encouraging with the women's team than with the men's. The men seemingly all had too much ego while the women tended to need or want a boost. Being more positive and encouraging really resonated with me as a much more enjoyable way to coach.

After only one season in that role, I left Williams to pursue a master's degree as a graduate assistant with the women's basketball program at Western Kentucky University. My journey includes two years at Western Kentucky, six years as an assistant and later Associate Head Coach at the College of the Holy Cross and eight years as head coach at Connecticut College, firmly entrenching myself in the world of coaching women.

As all good coaches do, I have spent a lot of time trying to make myself better, reading books & articles, listening to podcasts, perusing websites, attending clinics, and talking to other coaches. Pat Summitt, Geno Auriemma, Anson Dorrance, Tony DiCicco, Bob Starkey, C. Vivian Stringer all have well-thumbed titles on my bookshelf or are bookmarked on my browser. From all of them, I am trying to figure out what many coaches are seeking to discover: how can I better connect with the women on my team? How can I motivate them? How can I get them to care more? To be better teammates? To be more competitive? To be more coachable? How can I more effectively coach the women on my team?

Over the course of my sixteen years in the profession, I have been attempting to piece together a comprehensive approach as to how to successfully coach the women on our teams. In *Hormones, Hair Elastics & Helmets*, Dr. LaCure helps answer some of the questions those of us who coach women have been asking. He has provided us with a research-based guide to, as the subtitle states, successfully coach female athletes. In a succinct, yet comprehensive manner, Dr. LaCure addresses everything from why most females join teams and play sports to the physical and psychological differences between males and females to gender-based differences in coaching women.

As I read a draft of *Hormones, Hair Elastics & Helmets*, I found myself reviewing much of what we do in our women's basketball program at Connecticut College. Is playing basketball at Connecticut College fun? Are we fostering an environment where we can help improve their skills without seeming overly critical? Are we spending enough time on team chemistry and dynamic? Are our players forming lasting relationships while at the same time improving their skills and growing as players? Are we emphasizing results or performance improvement? Are they confident that we care about them as people?

This book will be a valuable addition to the libraries of those coaches who are asking similar questions; who are on a mission to more effectively coach their female athletes. After exploring some of the fundamental truths about female athletes, Dr. LaCure spends the remainder of the book laying out the *how* for us: how to encourage involvement and skill development, how to enhance self-confidence and how to foster team cohesion, to name a few.

Most importantly, however, Dr. LaCure reminds us of the *why*: that we coach with the desire to make a positive impact and add value to the lives of young women. We hope that we can encourage their confidence to grow and watch them develop meaningful relationships over the course of their time in sport. As Dr. LaCure says, our female athletes are "looking for coaches who are immensely talented and deeply caring. They are looking for coaches who are passionate about coaching and who will help them become better people, on and off the court." That is a lofty standard for every coach entrusted with a team of females but one to which we must continually aspire.

Brian Wilson
Head Women's Basketball Coach
Connecticut College

ACKNOWLEDGMENTS

I want to thank my parents. Thank you, Mom, for always reminding me that I can do anything, so long as I put my mind to it. I'm not sure if she was talking about coaching, but her words of advice did not fall on deaf ears. My father, while not into organized sports, was a good athlete. He loved to run and was inspired by outdoor activities. He loved to hunt and fish and I still enjoy the gift of fishing today.

A warm thank you goes to Joe Minihan. Together we have coached some great kids and felt the highs and lows that only being a coach can bring. You are a great coach, a tremendous role model for children, and a dear friend.

A big thank you to Rita Atkinson. Always loved coaching with you and most importantly appreciate your big heart and time you gave to let me vent. I also want to thank Andrew Pittington for his time, friendship and outstanding coaching stories. I would also like to thank Tim Brillo for his support and friendship. A special thank you to Rachel Sutton for quarterbacking this project to print.

I give special thanks to my four children, Ben, Michael, Madison, and Savannah. You truly inspire me daily to be the best and to do my best. You are the foundation of my coaching philosophy as I proudly share to families that "I will coach your child like I would want you to coach my children…with dignity, compassion and class." Additionally, a very heart-felt thank you to my son Ben. You are the best assistant coach around. You have made coaching even more special. Finally, Amanda Jean, thank you for coming up with the title of this book. I appreciate your constant prodding to get this book published.

I have been blessed to coach over 600 young men and women over the last twenty years. I thank them for making me a better coach, but more important, a better man. I have experienced many of the joys and challenges of coaching high school and college athletics. My coaching career began with the Lincoln-Sudbury boy's junior-varsity basketball team. I can still remember my first game. I was twenty-seven years old.

It was very exciting and I loved being on the sideline. My first game was against Marlboro High School. They were a very athletic team and we were talented and deep. I remember having only two weeks to run tryouts, select a team and "teach" them an offense and defense. I had never formally coached before so I relied heavily on my high school varsity coach, George Horton. He was heavy into man-to-man defense and the flex offense. I enjoyed pressing, trapping, and double-teaming wherever possible. So with only two weeks of formal coaching under my belt, we played the game. I felt like a spectator. The game was fast, players were moving all over the court and I felt as if I could not keep up with them. They always seemed to be one play ahead. However, I felt such pure joy and excitement. I was coaching. I was on the sideline and this was my team. I knew at that moment that coaching was something I loved and wanted to do…needed to do.

At halftime we had a large lead, not because of anything in particular I did, but because my team was talented and understood the game. They moved well without the ball and they could flat out play defense. So, even though I was unsure what to say or what adjustments to make during halftime, one thing was clear. However, after two weeks of practice and a sixteen minute half, I was hooked. This was for me.

For all of you who have had the great privilege to coach, you get it. Coaching is unlike any other career or vocation. You must be highly committed and in some small, yet significant way, you must be a bit crazy. Crazy to deal with the challenging parents, rescheduled games, and practices cancelled due to weather. Yet, we do it and we do it with pride, poise, and passion. Hopefully, this book will allow us all to do it a little better and a little wiser.

CHAPTER 1

MORE THAN JUST A GAME

///

"Be prepared and be honest."
~ John Wooden

Since the passage of Title IX in 1972, female athletic participation has increased dramatically. Title IX requires that any school that receives federal funding must have gender equity in their athletic programs. This includes having comparable equipment, fields, and access to similar sports (Stewart, 2001). While much has been done to ensure that female athletes are given the same athletic rights as their male counter-parts, little has been done to fully understand and appreciate why female athletes participate in athletics. Yes, there has been some scholarly work that explores why female athletes compete, but rarely do the results end up in comprehensive coaching education or mentoring programs. A review of the literature does demonstrate that numerous studies have been completed that explore how female athletes view participation in athletics, including what coaching style they find most beneficial. There does appear to be a void in the literature, however, that blends together a comprehensive look at how to successfully coach female athletes. *The Art and Science of Successfully Coaching the Female Athlete,* serves to fill that void.

A growing number of state-sponsored athletic associations have recognized the need for comprehensive coaches education programs and either offer them as a condition of coaching or provide them as a yearly, continuing education program. Some schools actually mandate that their coaches are certified through national or state-sponsored certification programs. The NFHS (The National Federation of High Schools) offers a national coaches certification program. Some states, however, have adopted their own coaches' certification programs as seen in Massachusetts for example (MIAA website, 2010). While these coaching certification programs are an excellent first step, they do not provide specific gender-based information such as the unique differences between coaching male and female athletes. They may include information about appropriate boundaries with athletes, avoiding sexual harassment, and protecting yourself as a coach by never being alone with an athlete; however, they rarely include detailed information about how female athletes approach competition. Or for that matter, they rarely include information about what type of coaching style is best suited for female athletes. As Doug Bruno, head women's basketball coach at DePaul University points out: "Nobody gave me a quickie course in gender differences when I got the job. I just walked on the floor and coached them like I would men. There is still no handbook" (Osbourne, 2002).

According to Steven Taylor (2000), female athletes list having fun, being with friends, and enjoying competition as the three primary reasons they participate in sports. However, male athletes list winning, competing, and teammates as their three primary reasons they participate. Since over eighty-one percent of coaches coaching female athletes are males, they may approach the motives for competing differently (Kenow, 1999). This has critical implications for all coaches of female athletes and for the development of any coaching education program. Kenow (1999) points out that the majority of high school and college athletes surveyed prefer having men as their coach. Some may question, however, if that is all they have been exposed to. Seemingly, they may feel more comfortable with a man, due to their lack of any direct experience with a female coach.

Upon a careful and thorough review of the literature, there does appear to be many important and significant differences in coaching female athletes. Some may have stayed away from publicly making that statement for fear that it might appear sexist. However, coaching education programs have not kept up with the rapid advancements of female athletics. There is a lack of traditional coaching books that deal specifically with the psychological differences between males and females.

As Caroline Silby (2000) points out, coaches, whether male or female, should be aware that female athletes want to develop personal relationships with their coaches. They prefer coaches who communicate openly and are empathic. Female athletes value friendship and like to focus on team unity. They place great value on personal improvement and prefer not to have their confidence challenged. To that end, few athletic programs offer coaches education programs; even fewer include detailed information and training about the differences between coaching male and female athletes.

Missing in most coaches training programs is a lack of information about how being either a male or female coach impacts the coach-athlete relationship. As Dr. Jack Levine, pediatrician and experienced youth coach points outs, coaches of adolescent girls have a great responsibility, beyond coaching the specific sport and winning games. They need to work hard to increase self-confidence and improve self-esteem. Their participation in youth sports should be a stepping stone to becoming self-assured, confident women (Silby, 2000).

As Osborne (2002) suggests, although male and female athletes share many attributes such as a desire to win, willingness to sacrifice time and energy, and the enjoyment of competition, most female athletes need to be coached differently. She also noted that most studies on the impact of coach gender have not utilized a qualitative approach. In order to develop an in-depth training program for coaches of female athletes, several questions need to be explored. First, how do female athletes respond to male and female coaches? Are there identifiable differences or are they less gender related and more style related? Furthermore, what does the world of athletics and competition look like through the eyes of the female athlete?

Few qualitative studies exist' that demonstrate how gender of the coach impacts the success of coaching female athletes. While there are numerous scholarly articles, papers and studies that examine the differences between coaching female and male athletes, far less exists in the literature that connects the impact of the gender of the coach with the gender of the athlete.

The role of the coach in the development of the whole person is enormous. With more and more female athletes participating in sports at a very high level, the need to understand how best to mentor and coach them grows in importance. For example, does the gender of the coach really play a role or is it more about the style of the coach, regardless of gender? Additionally, what role does being an athlete who is female play in the motivation, teaching, and development of her athletic career? Ultimately, coaches who instruct female athletes, regardless of level, need to have a greater understanding of how their gender impacts the relationship, coupled with a unique understanding of the challenges and joys that all coaches face in working with female athletes.

Are female athletes motivated by more than just winning and pure success? How are female athletes motivated, and what coaching style provides them with the necessary tools to succeed? Much of the research suggests that female athletes, regardless of level or skill are primarily motivated to have fun (Silby, 2000). That said, what do coaches need to understand about their female athletes to help them achieve the balance between winning, individual success, and enjoyment? Female athletes have a unique set of needs that address various issues specific to women (Smisk, 1996). Furthermore, Silby (2000) points out that many female athletes report that their coaches can really make playing fun or drain the fun out of competing. For that critical reason, all coaches of female athletes need to understand the specific coaching attributes that seem to work most successfully with female athletes, including understanding specific gender influences.

Osborne (2002) suggests that very little is known about the extent to which female athletes prefer a same-sex or opposite-sex coach. However, in addition to that shortage in the literature, it still remains that there are practical differences to coaching women. What are the physical and psychological differences, and what does it mean for the role of the coach and the nature of their relationship? As Smisek (1996) suggests, all players, male or female, must possess a combination of knowledge of the game, skill, ability, fitness, and training. However, looking beyond the technical aspects of the sport, it does appear that gender of both the coach and athlete plays a critical role in the emotional and physical success of the athlete and team.

The term "coaching" has a very specific and detailed meaning. Coaching as a concept has left the athletic fields and is now seen in corporate America as well as many mental health practices. More and more mental health practitioners utilize coaching as a brief and effective way to help someone successfully manage day-to-day living. Life coaches have grown in popularity and are even called upon in the corporate world to help businesses become more productive. The term "coaching" will be utilized within solely as it relates to athletics and athletes. Furthermore, "coaches" will be defined as those who are involved professionally with athletes, such as at the middle school, high school, collegiate or professional level. This is not to exclude the importance of youth coaching and those who give generously of their time, but the youth level deals mostly with parents volunteering their time rather than those professionals who have dedicated their lives and countless sleepless nights to properly prepare their athletes to compete. This is not to exclude youth sports or the millions of children who have participated over the years. Instead, a purposeful narrowing of the field to only include athletes at the highest levels. However, specific information will be presented about the role of youth coaches and their impact on youth athletic programs. This will serve to reinforce information rather than to provide comparisons.

PART II

Coaching Male and Female Athletes:

The Similarities and the Differences

"Not Just One of the Boys"

CHAPTER 2

PHYSICAL DIFFERENCES

"The key to winning is preparation, be prepared to win."
~ John Wooden

According to Bachir (2008), until puberty, girls and boys do not significantly differ in most measurements of body size or composition. On average, the process of puberty takes about four years in both sexes, although girls tend to enter puberty first. At puberty, body composition begins to shift dramatically. Estrogen causes increased fat deposits in females, especially in the hip and thigh area. Bones also grow at an increased rate at this time, although girls reach their final height sooner than boys (Wilmore, 2008).

According to Silby (2000), during puberty, conditioning for females should be less intense and weight training should be used less than with males during the same time. The extent to which boys and girls retain fat is related to the amount of exercise they get.

Women's fat tissue tends to distribute around their buttocks and breasts, whereas in boys, it may develop around the abdomen, face or breast tissue.

Male and female athletes do not differ in their lower body strength, which appears related to their fat-free mass. Females, however, do have less upper-body strength than males relative to their fat-free mass. The majority of a woman's mass is below her waistline (Wilmore, 2008). According to Bachir (2008), women reach their peak in strength by age 20 and men reach it between the ages of 20 and 30. On average, a female's strength is two-thirds that of a male.

Muscle growth is regulated mainly by testosterone, which is seen almost ten times in men than women. In general, women have twenty percent less muscle mass. However, when strength is measured in terms of lean body weight, this difference is greatly reduced (Gossilin, 2007). While increased testosterone leads to wider shoulders in males, estrogen, which is produced in much greater amounts in women, results in wider hips for women. Women generally have twenty to twenty-six percent fat tissue and men fall within fifteen to twenty percent (Silby, 2000). Women generally have smaller, less dense bones and begin growing two years earlier than men due to hormones.

According to Earle (2008), males and females have similar cardiac output as they advance through puberty. While males' hearts are bigger than females' hearts, they are proportional to body size and mass. After puberty, a female's cardiac potential is seventy to seventy-five percent to that of a male's. Women have a thirty percent lower concentration of hemoglobin, which is the primary system by which oxygen is transported through the body. As a result, a woman's cardiovascular system is thirty percent smaller than a man's (Smisek, 1996). One of the more obvious physical differences between male and female athletes, particularly as they enter puberty, is the onset of menstruation for females. According to Costill (2008), pre-menstrual symptoms may cause a drop in performance. These symptoms may include mood changes, fluid retention, bloating, and abdominal pain. The greatest difference, however, may be the female athlete triad.

The female athlete triad is comprised of disordered eating, osteoporosis, and Amenorrhoea. Disordered eating, while seen in male athletes, particularly wrestlers and gymnasts (Silby, 2000) is far more common in female athletes. Disordered eating can involve an effort to restrict calories in an attempt to maintain optimal physical health or other, far more severe eating disorders such as anorexia or bulimia. Osteoporosis involves the weakening of the bones over time, frequently by overuse and poor nutritional habits. Amenorrhoea is frequently caused by over-training, combined with drastic and unhealthy reductions in body fat (Earle, 2008). Being a highly competitive female athlete and participating in a sport that requires athletes to train is a key risk factor. Participation in sports where a specific low weight may be required can also place women at risk for developing the female athlete triad (Bachir, 2008).

Some of the risk factors of the female athlete triad include weight loss, no/irregular periods, fatigue, decreased ability to concentrate, stress fractures, and muscle injuries (Kenny, 2008). It has been estimated that over sixty percent of female athletes will experience some symptoms of disordered eating (Earle, 2008). With staggering numbers like this, it is critical that all coaches of women are mindful and watchful for any symptoms. Eating disorders can be very difficult to overcome and at their worst, they can be fatal (Earle, 2008).

According to Costill (2008), female athletes are six times more likely to experience knee injuries. Their smaller bone structure and extra fat mass makes their knee joints more vulnerable. Men tend to produce more sweat and start sweating earlier during activity than women. According to Bachir (2008), this may be an advantage for men in a hot, dry environment. However, dehydration can also be a potential problem.

Comparing purely physical attributes of men and women reveal that men have an advantage because of greater muscle mass, heart and lung capacity, and aerobic capacity.

These qualities generally give the average man more strength, power, and speed compared with the average woman. Women, however, are superior in flexibility and buoyancy (Wilmore, 2008).

It was once believed that women were not capable of performing at the same level as men; however, there is growing evidence that with proper training women can produce the aerobic capacity of trained men.

The greater muscle mass that males possess permits greater strength, power, and speed; however, prior to the onset of puberty, men and women are similar (Kenny, 2008). As Pat Croce, President of Sports Physical Therapists Inc., shared, those who have seen women experience natural childbirth know that the myth of women as the weaker sex is simply that – a myth (Wilmore, 2008).

CHAPTER 3

Psychological Differences
"It's Not All in Your Head"

"Make sure team members know they are working with you, not for you."
~ John Wooden

According to Gosselin (2002), boys in general play sports out of the individual need for competition. On the other hand, girls tend to be motivated by pleasing others and are more relationship oriented. Women are more willing to try new things – particularly if it makes them perform better. Women tend to work harder to please their coaches, whereas men tend to work harder to please themselves (Wilmore, 2008).

Prior to puberty, girls and boys seem to play sports for many of the same reasons. They want to have fun. They feel a need to belong to a group, have a desire to compete, and are interested in mastering skills involved in the sport in which they are participating. However, even as early as pre-school there are differences in the way male and female children interact. Garcia (2000) showed that pre-school girls interact in a cooperative, sharing manner while boys interacted in a competitive, individualized and, egocentric manner when learning fundamental motor skills. In addition, both girls and boys tried to maintain their gender style of interaction when dealing with the opposite sex. These differences in behavioral styles become increasingly more apparent with the onset of puberty and the continued process of maturation.

A 1999 study by the American Association of University Women (AAUW) revealed that sixty percent of elementary school girls are happy with who they are, yet, only twenty-nine percent of high school girls feel the same way. In a later AAUW study (2001) they found that as children progress through schools, boys perform better academically and feel better about themselves. Girls, however, saw their self-esteem, opinions of their gender, and scores on standardized achievement tests all decline. Girls place a greater value on what others think compared to boys (Gosselin, 2002).

In a study by Silby (2000), he found that women do not give them-selves enough credit for the things they do well. Women tend to base confidence on what others think of them rather than relying on internal sources of confidence. Women tend to be more open and forthcoming when feeling at their least confident. They are less inhibited to show lack of confidence in their body language and words. Women tend to need more of an ego boost, whereas for men, the opposite can often be true (Willmore, 2008). Confidence appears to be the central ingredient for all athletic success, regardless of gender.

In a follow-up study, Garcia (2001) found that female athletes tend to take coaches' criticisms personally and are more sensitive to com-ments directed at them. Male athletes demonstrated a greater ability to not let a coach's negative criticism impact them. Female athletes seem to spend more time internalizing negative feedback and expressing a need to "clear the air" more frequently.

Related to self-esteem issues is the extent to which girls value rela-tionships. Girls place a greater value on what others think of them and how they will fit into the group. Much of their satisfaction from par-ticipating in sports is gained from the relationships that they form on a team. According to Silby (2000), female standing is determined by their ability to connect and maintain relationships—acceptance, for men is determined by ability, and how well they can do things. In many ways, the standard that judges men by what they can do and women by how they look still exists in a powerful and meaningful way.

Girls view their teammates as friends. Team chemistry is very important to female athletes. Women will look for ways to enhance team bonding. Thus, when there are team issues, this can be both disruptive and distracting. According to Garcia (2001), girls tend to hold grudges longer which will influence their interactions with each other and negatively influence team chemistry. Boys, on the other hand, view their teammates as people with whom they play a sport. Boys tend to be more individualistic. Unlike girl's teams, boy's teams can function well even if the players are not friends. Boys have a greater ability to put their personal relationships on hold when competing. Girls place their performance in the context of team performance. Boys, however, have a tendency to externalize their performance from that of the team and are more likely to place blame on others for the team's performance rather than to take responsibility for it themselves (Gosselin, 2002). On the other hand, other studies such as the one conducted by Kenney (2008) suggests that a shift is occurring.

More and more female athletes, particularly those at the varsity high school and collegiate levels are pointing fingers at teammates rather than looking at where they made a mistake. In some way, female athletes are beginning to adopt competition styles historically only seen in traditional male sporting behavior and teams. It can be concluded that this style and approach is not particularly productive or valuable for either gender nor is it a style that works for most coaches (LaCure, 2012).

According to Gosselin (2002), in general boys play sports out of a need for competition. However, the need to compete seems to be a critical factor in why girls participate, too. In fact, more and more girls are playing organized sports, and more and more girls care about the final score. To suggest that girls play sports only to bond, connect, and be part of a team is short-sighted and narrowly defined. In fact, girls do seek out athletic competition for all of the same reasons that boys do. The primary difference is that girls tend to care far more about how their coaches, parents, and teammates view them. They hold onto criticism longer than boys and they need to know they are valued by everyone on their team. They value the emotional connections between players and between their coaches. However, at the end of the game, they still value winning just as much as boys.

Female athletes may face challenges in relating to each other. Wiseman (2002) describes a social hierarchy among girls that develops as they strive for popularity during their transition from girls to women. Relationships mean everything to adolescents, but especially for girls because of internal struggles they have with self-esteem. Both boys and girls can be mean and aggressive, but they frequently do so in different ways. Boys tend to be physically mean, whereas girls generally lash out in words, gestures, and body language. Wiseman (2002) describes that status is acquired in a variety of ways including the use of exclusion of some while showing favoritism toward others. The overall behavior results in a powerful dynamic among young girls that includes the formation of cliques. Boys have similar types of structures, but their athletic performance is not as dependent upon relationships with each other as they are with girls. Coaches need to be aware of this potential road block to success and work very hard to take steps to minimize its impact. Additionally, coaches need to be careful that they do not show favor, perceived or otherwise to some players at the exclusion of others. Female athletes will notice and there will be an impact on total team chemistry (LaCure, 2012).

It appears that boys have been raised to compete whereas girls have been raised to cooperate. These family and societal factors creep into every athletic or team situation. Girls are still being raised to please while boys are being raised to become strong and independent. While this progression seems to be changing, boys and girls are still being raised to view competition in different ways. Ironically, in Pollack's ground-breaking book, *Real Boys,* he suggests that while there has been steady improvement in opportunities for girls, boys are sadly losing ground. Boys have lower national test scores than girls in high school and higher suicide rates. Pollack (2002) points out that when boys are raised only to compete, they frequently burn out or are eaten up when they can't keep up with their peers. Are girls headed for the same fate?

As more girls are being raised to value competition and view their female peers as competitors rather than cohorts, we are seeing a decrease in team unity and cohesiveness. The drive to be successful athletically appears to provide the potential consequence of a "me first" player, focused more on her goals, rather than that of the team. Are we raising female athletes to ignore their need for team unity in order to capture their individual athletic goals?

During my 2011-2012 basketball season, I had a talented sophomore player fall into this trap. She had some very solid offensive skills and was a competent shooter. She seemed to enjoy playing the game, and spending time with her friends on the team. However, after injuring her ankle and the subsequent rehab, she did not return to her same role on the team as the first sub off the bench. While skilled on the offensive end, she lacked the toughness and technique on the defensive side of the ball. While she did play in every game and received solid minutes, she was not happy. Rather than working harder in practice or standing out defensively, her attitude began to fall. At one point her father actually emailed me to suggest that his daughter should not only be playing more, but that she should be a starter and selfishly pointed out the players who he felt his daughter was better than. As a coach for over twenty-five years, that short-sighted email from a short-sighted parent did not surprise me. What surprised me occurred during a player-coach meeting with this student-athlete. She proceeded to tell me why she should be starting and who she was more talented than. I had never had a player be that direct, honest or *selfish* before.

It reminded me that the female athlete *is* changing. She is more concerned with *her* playing time and *her* individual accomplishments. More and more, the female athlete and her family have their eyes on playing at a top Division 1 college, highly recruited and paid for. This reflects a critical shift in female athletics and radically changes the motivation for many women and girls to participate and compete. It also represents an important time for all coaches of female athletes.

CHAPTER 4

WHAT MOTIVATES THE FEMALE ATHLETE TO PARTICIPATE OR COMPETE?

"An eagerness to sacrifice personal interests or glory for the welfare of all."
~ John Wooden

Research suggests that women and girls participate in sports and physical activities for many varied reasons. Frequently, female athletes are attracted to sports for the elements of affiliation, skill development, personal improvement, a nurturing environment, and a social network (Sturrock, 1999). Many female athletes still report that some barriers to participate still exist. For example, some athletes feel there has been a lack of encouragement, lack of opportunity, or conflict with other activities. Many have the belief that they do not have the skill set to participate and parents who perpetuate stereotypes by associating sport with masculinity (Feltes, 2000). According to Lehmann (2003), female athletes report that they value the enjoyment of competition and making friends through sport. In addition, most female athletes report that participation in athletics is a great way to stay in shape, reduce stress, and have fun. Sturrock (1999) interviewed hundreds of female athletes participating in collegiate sports and found that often, one's closest friends are teammates. In addition, Sturrock noted that athletes report that the confidence level of the team increases when the athletes know each other well and when they know each other's abilities. Furthermore, when coaches allow for some social time, female athletes seem to report a better focus in practice and games.

Social interaction and team dynamics seem to be features that attract females to participation in athletics. Team members spend a great deal of time together over the course of the season. It is the camaraderie and social networking that causes many females to participation in sports. Team cohesion can greatly enhance the enjoyment athletes experience through participation, as well as their performance. As a result, it is important for coaches and parents to encourage the development of positive and energy-enhancing team dynamics, even in sports where athletes compete individually (Stewart, 2001). Unlike the parent and player who placed their individual needs well above the team and created an atmosphere of tension and peer-conflict, parents need to encourage healthy team dynamics. In fact, they need to demand it.

According to Sturrock (2000) girls should be given the opportunity to socialize; girls seem to need this component more than boys. The practice of team dinners and other team activities that promote bonding and team unity seem to pay immediate dividends in how female athletes enjoy the season. It would appear that the decades-long practice of bringing players together outside of competition may actually help them to perform better. At a minimum, it is clear that one of the primary motivations for women and girls to participate in athletics, beyond competition, is to create and develop relationships. Coaches at all levels need to be mindful of this important revelation and are charged with taking responsibility for the social dynamics of the team. Coaches can't make everyone get along all the time, but they can make sure that they provide the time to try.

As female athletics continues to evolve, grow, and change, one must notice how women's athletics are beginning to take on the national stage. In March of 2012, the Women's Division 1, National Basketball

Championship was one of the most watch games in collegiate history. With millions of viewers world-wide, female athletics is a growing money-maker for colleges, universities, and networks. As a result, the recruiting process for high profile female athletes for high profile teams is growing. As you might expect, also watching are parents and their daughters hoping that they might be the next National Champions on ESPN.

As a result, more and more female athletes are specializing in one sport at earlier and earlier ages. They now play the sport year round and frequently participate in elite leagues, AAU and other non-school sanctioned programs in the hopes that they too will play on a Sunday night in March, in primetime, on ESPN.

High school coaches need to be wary that many of their players are no longer focused only on their school team, but now have many other teams to participate with and chase the dream, or maybe the dream of their parents. As a result, more and more parents and their daughters are expressing concern that their high school coach is interfering with their chance to play at "the next level." It is not uncommon for parents to offer unsolicited suggestions to high school coaches as to what position their daughters should play to get the best chance for exposure and a scholarship. Almost every high school coach surveyed would report that one of the top motivations for girls to participate in high school athletics is shifting—shifting from the desire to compete and make lifetime connections, to the pure desire to play at the next level and to do it…for free.

PART III

Coaching Female Athletes

CHAPTER 5

Does the Gender of the Coach
Make a Difference?

*"A man may make mistakes but he isn't a failure
until he starts blaming someone else."*
~ John Wooden

The leadership styles that coaches use to motivate men and women are as varied as they are distinct. According to Anson Dorrance (2001), female athletes want to see their coaches as human. They need to know that they have a connection with the coaches and that their coaches care about them as people. With males, however, consistently successful male coaches usually have strong personalities who lead with a powerful presence and will. Male coaches usually involve power and influence as part of their personalities. A coach of male athletes has to convince their team that their vision is correct. On the contrary, women seem to be willing to consider a coach's vision and try it before judging it. This does seem to be evolving and changing for the female athlete, however, as it is more the rule for female athletes to question the coach rather than to give unconditional approval to their requests or game-planning decisions (LaCure, 2012). Males typically do not need a personal relationship as long as there is respect, but with women, a personal relationship is at the core foundation of success. According to Smisek (2002), you basically have to drive men, but you can lead women…the way you coach women is a more civilized model of leadership.

A critical component for males coaching female athletes, especially during adolescence, is that while boys and girls may be raised in the same household and apparently the same cultural environment, they are influenced by many subtle and not so subtle ways As pointed out in the book, *The Gendered Society,* Kimmel (2000) claims that the seeds of gender difference are first established in the family. This is where boys receive their first messages about what it means to be a male and where girls first learn what it means to be a female. Although many do not realize it, parents possess a set of gender-specific beliefs about what boys and girls should be like at various ages. A powerful consequence of this is that, in general, boys are encouraged to be more independent and are played with more roughly whereas many more limits are placed on the acceptable behavior of the girls and they are treated more gently. Ultimately, girls are taught to capitalize on their external features and seek approval from others. Contrarily, boys discover that their athletic ability and individual performances are important to succeed as a male. Girls are rewarded for their looks and for being attractive, while boys are rewarded for their physical performance and for being active (Silby, 2000).

Ultimately, no female athlete or female sports teams ever win any trophies, medals or state championships for how they look; rather, they are rewarded for their accomplishments. Tournament seedings are based upon record, not beauty; skill not looks. Gender influences are critical for all coaches of women to understand and if at all possible, to change for the better.

While the focus of this book is not to explore all of the factors that influence gender identity, it is important for coaches to understand how their gender might impact their role as coaches. Do men coach women differently? Should they coach women differently? What messages did the coach receive growing up about gender and gender roles? Smisek

(1998) suggests that more important than gender of the coach or athletes is the coach's ability to teach the game. What seems to be most important is: Can the coach provide general team management that permits all athletes with the opportunities to improve skills and build self-esteem, while developing well-organized, challenging practices? Silby (2000) indicates that a specific athlete may respond better to a male while another may respond better to a female coach. It is not a male versus female coach issue at all. Instead, it is critical for coaches of both genders to understand the female sports perspective. Silby (2000) adds, "Coaches, whether male or female, should be aware that female athletes…want to develop personal relationships with them and prefer coaches who communicate openly and are empathic. Female athletes value friendship and like to focus on team unity. They place high value on personal improvement and prefer not to have their confidence attacked."

Male coaches to varying degrees are products of their environments in which they were raised. As a product of their environments, male coaches may have certain expectations about how athletes should perform and what it takes to motivate them. Males also communicate differently than females (Gray, 2001). A mistake many male coaches make is that they try to motivate with the intensity of their own personalities (Dorrance, 1999). All males have experienced aggressive, loud, in-your-face motivational speeches from coaches or constant yelling as a way to drive them. Although this approach is not advocated for either male or female athletes, male athletes frequently respond to this type of motivational strategy. However, this type of communication style is generally not productive when it comes to coaching female athletes. In fact, this type of coaching style will probably quickly erode their confidence, self-esteem, and the desire to compete.

According to Mark Stevenson (2004), the most important factor for men to understand in coaching women's athletics is that the male coach can't look at them as women. Instead, he needs to look at them as athletes. Stevenson adds that as long as you look at women as athletes, you will treat them as athletes. Steven Murray (2007) suggests that gender of the coach should not be a factor in determining who the next coach should be. Murray states, "Philosophically, it is very pernicious to even remotely consider the gender of an individual for a coaching job. When one does this, one immediately assumes that one gender is superior to the other gender in coaching. This is wrong and definitely a form of discrimination, and as such, cannot be tolerated."

It could be argued that if men should only coach boys and women should only coach girls, then boys should only have male teachers and girls should only have female teachers. Few could argue that having meaningful, caring adults of both genders in the lives of student-athletes is a bad thing. In fact, having role models, including coaches and teachers of both genders can only enrich the world of the student-athlete. Not only can female athletes benefit greatly from having men as coaches but it also gives women the opportunity to coach males at the highest levels. The premise that women should only coach women and men are naturally better coaches needs to be revised and updated. Clearly men are wonderful coaches and role-models for young women; however, just as clear is that women are tremendous mentors and coaches for young men.

It is often noted in the research that male and female athletes prefer having a male as a coach. Eighty percent of all coaches at the high school and collegiate level are male. At the collegiate level, only two percent of the coaches of men's teams and less than half of the coaches of women's teams are female (Acosta, 2006). One of the arguments traditionally about why it is better to have a man as a head coach is that women are not winning championships. When explored fully, however, more female coaches are coaching mid-major programs rather than the elite, highly paid Division I programs (Acosta, 2006). In addition, the myth is that female coaches do not have the leadership skills or cannot be tough enough to command respect. According to Carpenter (2006), athletes, regardless of gender, report that they respect coaches who are highly organized, prepared, and skilled in the sport they are teaching.

It is not unusual to encounter situations where male or female athletes express a preference for male coaches, especially after a well-liked male coach leaves a program.

Research demonstrates that female athletes who have never had a female coach believe that male coaches are better than female coaches. Male and female athletes may have been taught to devalue the athletic abilities of females and may believe that female coaches cannot coach as well as males. Some male athletes may worry that their friends and opposing teams will tease them if they have a female as a head coach. Because so few women coach men, people may not be sure how to react (Glesne, 2004).

Numerous studies have examined the impact of gender on the coach-athlete relationship. An athlete's preference for same-sex or opposite-sex coaches have been examined, and factors taken into consideration have included level of knowledge and ability to motivate and capability of being a role model (Simmons, 2006). Molstad (2007) found that female basketball players ranked female coaches as superior in the coaching qualities of relating well to others and understanding athletes' feelings (two of the three most important rated qualities), while no difference was found among other characteristics. Conversely, however, a strong sex bias favoring male coaches was found in male and female high school basketball players who rated male coaches as more knowledgeable, more likely to achieve future success, more desirable to play for, and having a greater ability to motivate (Williams, 2005). Overall, eighty-nine percent of male athletes and seventy-one percent of female athletes preferred a male coach. Previous research investigations have not demonstrated a clear consensus for coach gender for female athletes (Smith, 2005).

Osborne (2002) suggested that although male and female athletes share many attributes such as desire to win and enjoyment of competition, athletes do not need to be coached differently. Of note, it appears that much of the research that has explored the impact of coach gender on the female athlete has been conducted quantitatively and has used hypothetical coaches (Williams, 2005). Few qualitative studies exist that explore female athletes' experience with actual male and female coaches, thus leaving a tremendous gap in the literature and need for further exploration.

In an extensive qualitative study by Frey (2007), she noted that female athletes felt that male coaches were more structured and organized. Furthermore, male coaches appeared more prepared, including developing detailed practice plans. Male coaches were seen as being harder on the athletes and expected more from their players than female coaches. Many athletes reported that there would be consequences to face in practices under a male coach if they did not pay attention or were not serious. Some of the athletes reported that they responded favorably to the coaches' disciplinary style but others found male coaches overly strict. Conversely, many of the respondents felt that female coaches were less organized and non-authoritative. Concerns that female coaches tended to run late and were not fully prepared for team success were noted, as well as a concern that practices were not structured nor on a consistent time schedule.

Many athletes perceived that female coaches had a harder time trying to accomplish goals in practice and did not seem to be as concerned about individual skill development. Frey (2007) found that female coaches had a greater tendency toward being friends with the players and getting to know more about them as players. In addition, she found that female coaches were more likely to provide encouraging, motivating comments, while male coaches were seen to provide more diverse feedback. Osborne (2002) found that the personal relationships between female athletes and male coaches are very different from the relationships with female coaches. Many female athletes report feeling intimidated by their male coaches, whereas they felt they could discuss almost anything with their female coaches. Most of the female athletes reported, however, that if their male coach was approachable and emotionally sensitive to their needs as a whole person, then they would be more likely to share non-sport related concerns with their coach.

Female athletes benefit from a personal connection with the coach.

When coaching females, there is a need for warmth, empathy, and a sense of humor (Burke, 2005). Female high school and collegiate basketball players ranked the coaching qualities of relating well to athletes and understanding athletes' feelings as two of the top three characteristics. Female coaches consistently rate higher than male coaches on demonstrating those qualities (Osborne, 2002). Simmons (2000) found that female athletes are more likely to disclose personal information to female coaches. As a result, female athletes reported feeling more connected to their female coaches. However, with that connection comes some significant hurdles.

According to Frey (2007), many female athletes feel that their female coaches tend to develop favorites and as a result, felt it impacted their ability to master a certain drill or skill. Present findings suggest that female coaches are viewed as more encouraging and motivating through a greater use of positive feedback. However, while many female athletes reported feeling more connected to their female coaches, many also reported that the closer relationship sometimes interfered. For example, if the coach needed to discipline a player for breaking team rules or not working hard, many female athletes reported that they had female coaches who were unable to follow through and let some players slide as to not interfere with the relationship. Many female athletes share that they appreciate the fact that most male coaches treated the *entire* team fairly, regardless of talent or individual relationship (Frey, 2007).

Female athletes tend to be more accepting of male coaches' mentality than that of the female coach. Women seem to prefer the authoritarian style of coaching used by male coaches. Women may prefer this style of coaching due to cultural expectations of men in authority positions, male dominance in women's sports or the lack of female coaches as role models (Osborne, 2002). However, if coaches use an extreme style such as constant yelling, female athletes will be less receptive to the authoritarian style (Frey, 2007).

According to Frey (2007), most female athletes who express a preference as to gender of their coach report preferring a male. Athletes cite factors such as greater level of knowledge, knowing what it takes to be successful, and having more respect for him. Some of the literature suggests that athletes may be more comfortable with male authority figures who demonstrate strong leadership and motivation skills (Molstad, 2005). Similarly, since men have historically held coaching positions for a longer period, athletes may have more confidence in their knowledge levels and coaching abilities (Sabock, 2000). According to Frey (2007), in the late 1980s and 1990s, much of the literature stated that the primary reason that female athletes preferred a male coach was because there was simply a shortage of women in the profession. It was believed that if female athletes were exposed earlier and more frequently to female coaches, then they would develop a preference for female coaches. However, this has not been the case. As the numbers of women entering the coaching profession in the 1990s and turn of the century increased substantially, the research still revealed that female athletes overwhelmingly preferred having a man as their coach. Caution should be taken in assuming that coach preference is only due to gender. Additional factors exist that may influence athletes' perceptions of coaches such as success of the team, or style of the current coach (Williams, 2001). Anxious players tend to report more negative perceptions of their coaches regardless of coach gender (Osborne, 2002). Parental feedback can also play a huge role in how female athletes view their coach, too.

If parents are supportive and positive about their daughters' coaches more often than not, the athletes' perceptions of the coach are positive, too. Conversely, if parents are negative about the coaches' abilities or coaching styles, then frequently, almost without fail, the athlete is as well (LaCure, 2010). Smith (2005) found that female athletes coached by women reported a greater desire to become head coaches. Other personal attributes such as athletes' age, socioeconomic status, ethnicity, and athletes overall skills impact the athletes' experience with coaches (Williams, 2005).

According to LaCure (2010), athletes who receive the majority of substantial playing time almost always report a good relationship with their coaches regardless of gender. Players who receive little or no play-ing time tend to report dissatisfaction with their coaches regardless of gender or coaching style. This is a critical factor for all coaches to con-sider as they try to understand the best style or approach to take with their teams. It appears that when an athlete is playing, he or she is gener-ally happy with their coach. While conversely, if he or she is not receiv-ing much playing time, his or her perception of the coach is generally impacted in a negative way. This could have tremendous implications for coaches as they consider how large of a team they select. Longitudi-nal studies should be conducted to more thoroughly examine the influ-ences that male and female coaches have on their athletes. However, what does seem to be very clear is that more than the coaches' gender is the coaches' style and ability to relate with and connect to athletes. Caring, knowledgeable coaches who have athletes playing substantial minutes are generally thought of positively by their teams, regardless of gender. While it appears that relationships are more important to female athletes, male athletes report valuing a coach who cared for them off the field, too.

Male coaches, just like the best fathers with their daughters, can have a tremendously positive influence on a female athlete's life that goes well beyond the sport. Male coaches, first and foremost, must coach the athlete and not the gender in the context of the skills, knowl-edge of the game, mental abilities, and fitness. Female athletes are capable of great success. As a result, it is critical for male coaches to recognize that there are inherent challenges in communicating with and understanding what motivates female athletes. All coaches must be aware of a female athlete's feelings and the relationships with them (Gos-slin, 2006). All coaches must understand completely how their gender and the gender of their players can impact the player-coach relationship. Coaches should be mindful of how gender roles are developed and how they continue to evolve over time. Gone thankfully are the days where girls played basketball in skirts and could not cross over the half court line. However, many of the harmful stereotypes remain regarding women participating in sports at the highest level. All coaches, male or female need to remember that not only are they coaches, mentors, and role models, but they are also agents for change. Through their behavior, on and off the field, they can elicit change and impact harmful stereotypes for both boys and girls. There can be no better motivation.

CHAPTER 6

THE COACH-ATHLETE RELATIONSHIP:
BUILDING TEAM CHEMISTRY

"A great athlete is one who considers the rights of others before her own feelings, and the feelings of others before her own rights."
~ John Wooden

The coach-athlete relationship has shown to have a profound effect on an athlete's satisfaction, performance, and quality of life (Greenleaf, 2001). Several factors may influence this relationship. Trust, friendship, and feedback from the coach have a positive impact on the performances of athletes who meet or exceed expectations. Athletes experiencing burnout have cited the coach as a negative influence due to the coaches' lack of belief in the athlete, extreme pressure, and/or unrealistic expectations (Taylor, 2001). Stewart (2000) found that athletes' perceptions of coaching competence and coaching behaviors were contributing factors to performance.

A girl's coach must understand that while males look for an action-oriented environment for competition, females prefer a more even approach. They want to be addressed in a friendly and respectful manner and are turned off by yelling, screaming, and the throwing of objects (Pendleton, 2007). Overbearing displays of emotion can create a hostile environment that could cause sensitive athletes to quit. Coaches who believe in yelling should do so only sparingly and should direct it at the group rather than the individual (Stewert, 2001). Selders (2003) suggests that winning for winning's sake is less important for the average female and that she is more goal-oriented than the typical male athlete. Coaches who thrive on winning at all costs may find they are not connecting with their female athletes. While female athletes want to win and greatly value winning, they are also focused on the team and team chemistry. Some coaches may struggle with the fact that while they are paid to win, their female athletes have additional and evolving priorities, too. Development of team chemistry is so important to female athletes that coaches who interfere with this process will find themselves on the outside looking in, wondering why they have lost the ear of their team.

Girls are also different from boys in their need for a nurturing, family-like camaraderie with teammates and coaches. It is important for them to feel close with their teammates and coaches and they may need to be motivated to succeed (Pendleton, 2007). For male teams, they receive much of their enjoyment largely on playing time and winning. Contrarily, the most enjoyable type of team for most females is a group of girls who gets along well, on and off the court (Selders, 2003). The teams that have the best camaraderie are usually the ones who are the most successful in terms of team unity and seasonal improvement.

As I reflect on the 2011-2012 basketball season, I witnessed first-hand how a few players who are not happy with their playing time can negatively impact the team camaraderie. Their impacts were so far reaching that many players sought me out to share their hope that I would not keep the unhappy players next season. Several of my players reported that their teammates' negative attitudes on the bench, in the locker room, and at practice began to impact their enjoyment of the season. While this team had a successful season in terms of skill development and record, many players at their end-of-the-season meeting with coaches reported that they did not enjoy the season as much as possible because of a breakdown in team cohesiveness. Ultimately it is up to coaches to provide the forum for players to make connections and develop relationships. One of the most effective, yet overlooked ways to do this is by keeping less players. If coaches keep fewer players then there are fewer players unhappy about their playing time. In turn, there are fewer distractions and more players who are focused on skill development and team camaraderie. We all have heard the famous quote "Misery loves company." It is critical that coaches try as hard as possible to keep players with positive attitudes, regardless of playing time or role on the team. I have heard my team…loud and clear.

Female athletes report that their coach plays a critical and important role in the development of strong team chemistry (Silby, 2002). The coach of female athletes needs to serve as a facilitator of good relationships on the team and must be vigilant to not pit players against each other in ways that will disrupt team unity or team chemistry. The role of team chemistry has different implications in female and male sports. Whereas it is an essential prerequisite for optimal performance in female sports, it is more a by-product of optimal performance among male teams (Pendelton, 2007). All of the literature suggests that all teams, regardless of gender, meet or exceed team goals if they are unified and feel collectively valued. The coach plays an important role in establishing these strong and positive team dynamics. According to Shurrock (2006), good coaches help their athletes learn not to judge one another based on their athletic ability. Great coaches model positive leadership and team-first skills, coupled with building the individual confidence of all of their players.

Many female athletes tend to have lower levels of confidence compared to men. Their confidence depends on three major components: nature of the task, need for clear and positive feedback, and social acceptance (Pendelton, 2007). To enhance a girl's self-perception, coaches must make sure she is comfortable with the nature of the task. She needs to feel like she has the ability to master the skill before she is asked to perform it at a competitive level.

Female athletes also need clear and positive feedback. Ambiguous, negative criticism will likely negatively impact their confidence. They are much more likely than boys to be disturbed by negative comments, and unlike boys, they will hold on to the feedback (Silby, 2002). All athletes, but particularly female athletes respond very well to positive feedback as well as praise and encouragement. The late John Wooden believed that coaches should seek out private moments to criticize athletes who need it, while seeking public moments to share the praise (Pendelton, 2007). Many coaches become too willing to criticize and too reluctant to give much-needed compliments. Most experienced coaches report that positive, verbal reinforcement is the key to success in coaching women (Pendleton, 2007).

According to Robert Selders (2008), studies have repeatedly demonstrated that female athletes prefer a friendly and more respectful atmosphere in which to train. They prefer a high level of camaraderie among players and between their coaches. They want to be around players and coaches who create a family-oriented team environment which effectively meets the needs of each of its players. Female athletes overwhelmingly prefer coaches who demonstrate warmth, empathy, and a sense of humor. They want to have a strong connection to their coach, yet they are wary of appearing like there is favoritism (Pendelton, 2007). Female athletes, as much as they want to feel connected to their coach, are concerned about appearing as if they are being favored by their coach. In fact, if they are being favored by their coach it can cause them discomfort as they are worried about how their teammates will view them. According to a study by Guylaine Demers (2004), both coaches and athletes attach more importance to the coach's personality than to his or her gender as a factor that determines how well a team bonds and connects.

CHAPTER 7

What Coaching Style Do Female Athletes Prefer? "Don't Give Up on Me Yet!"

"Don't let what you cannot do get in the way of what you can do."
~ John Wooden

According to Margaret Kalaska (2008), female athletes prefer a coaching style that creates a fun environment so that athletes can experience success and skill development. Additionally, female athletes want to be involved with coaches who create physical challenges that allow them to positively experience their athletic capabilities. In order for female athletes to achieve optimal performance, they need a coach who will state their expectations upfront. They want a coach who will explain mistakes rather than merely pointing them out (Babbitt, 2004). All athletes, but particularly female athletes, want a coach who maintains a positive attitude and treats players in a positive way. Coaches need to be approachable if athletes want to talk about the sport or something in their personal lives that may be affecting their performance or attitude (Silby, 2004).

According to Lisa Zimmerman, author of *Raising Our Athletic*

Daughters, "Children want to feel good about themselves through accomplishment. The crucial element of self-worth is not consistent success, but experience of progressing, becoming better, succeeding where you have failed." According to Kyla Heibert, Women's Basketball Coach for the University of Wisconsin, "The coach's first words set the tone for the whole season" (Longman, 2008). Female athletes want coaches who respect their abilities and understand the different personalities within the team. Female athletes seem to respond better to coaches who spend relatively equal time and attention with athletes in order to avert charges of favoritism (Silby, 2008).

According to Dee Dee Haight, alpine skiing coach for the University of Colorado, "Favoritism is a huge concern for female athletes. If one girl has an abundance of talent and the coach spends a great deal of time with her, the others will think this athlete is getting too much attention" (Kenow, 2007). Conversely, sometimes athletes who are doing well don't seem to require as much help and face neglect. It is imperative to balance your time between your athletes so they perceive equity and fairness.

Female athletes are concerned that they have a coach who will not let them get down on themselves. Furthermore, female athletes prefer a coach who has a good sense of humor, and uses encouraging words while giving honest feedback. Female athletes want feedback as to why they are playing a certain position and what they can do to receive more playing time. Additionally, female athletes are more likely to internalize emotional issues and as a result, need a coach who is genuine and approachable (Campbell, 2009). According to Marley Harris (2006), coaches need to emphasize that performance in sports doesn't define or determine one's self-worth.

According to Silby (2002), female athletes value coaches who have teams fill out goal sheets. They want to be challenged in practice and if they have a poor game or get emotional, respect their space. However, be available to encourage and support them in a positive way when they are ready to talk.

According to Anson Dorrance (2005), Women's Soccer Coach for the University of North Carolina, making connections with her coach is very important to the female athlete. She wants a coach who develops a different relationship with each player.

Some women don't want any kind of connection, while others require a closer, more caring relationship. Some want consistent feedback; some do not want any at all. However, it must be a relationship of their choosing. They will let coaches know what they need, or don't and it is the coach's responsibility to be prepared and to respond.

As much as one might believe that all athletes value public praise, for the female athlete, this public praise can sometimes make them uncomfortable. In addition, they worry about how their teammates will view them after this praise. Research suggests that their teammates may wonder why they did not receive praise, too (Dorrance, 2005). Female athletes value coaches who value them. Research suggests that female athletes overwhelmingly prefer a positive coaching style; however, they do expect and appreciate constructive feedback.

Women want to know what they did right in addition to what they did wrong. Yelling and constant negative feedback will cause the female athlete to tune-out the coaches' comments, no matter how well-founded or accurate they might be. Coaches of female athletes may need to praise female athletes and convince them they can be successful and that they have the skills to be successful. Sometimes coaches have to be a salesperson to help female athletes believe in their own abilities (Lehmann, 2004).

Female athletes do not want individualized pressure. They are much more comfortable with the pressure and expectations being place upon them by the team. Many female athletes report if pressure is placed on one particular athlete and she fails, she feels like she has let herself, team, and coach down. Female athletes want a coach who believes in the team, rewards the team for effort, and has high expectations and standards for the team (Lehmann, 2004). All coaches of female athletes and teams need to recognize how much their players want them to have realistic but high standards for them as individuals and as a team as a whole.

Athletes want to know that you believe in them and you believe in their abilities. They want you to set a tone of excellence and they want you to live it every practice, every game, and every day, on and off the field.

It appears that most female athletes prefer a coach who is caring, genuine, talented, and knows the game they are teaching. Female athletes want a coach who can motivate them and teach them, nurture and care about them. As Jodi Campbell, a Division I basketball player shared in a recent interview, "My coach cared so much about basketball, the team and us as individual players, that I would have run through a cement wall for him if he told me it would make me a better player. We didn't so much ask why he asked us to do something. We just believed that he knew it was right and he cared about us…so we did it" (Dorrance, 2009). All coaches should take away that if you demonstrate that you care and you are good at teaching the game, your players will run through a wall for you. Much more enjoyable than banging your head against the wall, wondering why your players go around the wall instead of through it.

PART IV

CHAPTER 8

The Role of Parents on Athletics
"Oh...If They Could All Be Orphans"

"Keep judgment and common sense."
~ *John Wooden*

There is a joke among American coaches that the best place to coach is a juvenile penal institution. Why? Three reasons: 1. No recruiting. 2. No away games and 3. No Parents. In some other coaching circles, when asked what is the best type of player to coach? The response is a quick and emphatic....Orphans. In a presentation at a national soccer coaches meeting a few years ago, then head coach of the USA Women's National Team, Anson Dorrance, was asked what it was like to have won the first Women's World Cup (in China). Wasn't he glad that he didn't have to deal with parents while coaching that team? He laughed and shared that after the awards ceremony in China, as he was leaving the field, he was approached by two sets of parents who had made the trip to watch their daughters compete. Expecting to hear additional congratulations, he was taken aback by being stripped by the parents because their daughters had not received enough playing time to justify their trip to China (Stewart, 2006). If it can happen at that level, it can happen anywhere...

and it does.

I will always remember my first win as a varsity basketball coach. I will remember it because it was my first win, and because one particular parent helped me to celebrate it. This was in the early 1990s and I was the boys' varsity basketball coach for Holliston High School. This was a school that in a period of five years had five different varsity coaches. I was number five. After starting off the season with two straight losses, we managed to secure my first win at home against Ashland High School. It was a back and forth game that we closed out with strong defense and some big foul shots. While leaving the court to address my team in the locker room, I received a nice round of congratulatory handshakes and "nice win coach." As I approached the locker room door, one parent stopped to grab my ear. I thought that he too would be congratulating me on the first of many wins. However, instead he wanted to know why his son was not in at the finish of the game. I was shocked. But, I was young, hopeful, and I thought everyone would be happy with the win. Instead, I found out that the win was secondary to his need to see his son play; his happiness was predicated on his son finishing the game rather than how well the team finished the game. I shared that while his son had played well offensively for us, his defensive effort was inconsistent and I needed my best defensive team in the game to protect the lead and close out the game. He walked away in anger and I walked into the locker room to address the team. I later found out this father was a minister. This exchange continues to remind me that no matter what a parent does for work, at the end of the day, they are a parent and they care more about their child and their child's playing time rather than the team or final score.

While many coaches report that managing parents is the greatest challenge to being a coach, there can be no refuting the important role parents play in female athletics. When their children were young, parents drove them to and from practice and games. When they needed hundreds of dollars to play on elite travel teams the parents shelled it out. When their child had the opportunity to play for the best teams or to be trained by the best coaches, the parents were there making it happen. However, what is also happening is that many parents feel as if they are now entitled to comment on coaching tactics, strategy, and most frequently…playing time.

Gone are the days where the majority of parents told their children, "Respect your coach and listen to what they have to say." Now we have a generation of athletes, young and old who question the coaches' decisions because at home, their parents are questioning them, too. Gone are the days when players played, parents parented, and coaches coached. Instead we are left with parents who yell instructions from the sidelines, because they once coached a youth team or participated in high school athletics. More and more, athletes are looking in the stands for approval and guidance rather than looking toward the bench for feedback from their coach. All professional coaches deal with this attitude and behavior on a daily basis. What used to be an occasional inconvenience is now the norm for most programs. In fact, parents are now so difficult to deal with that most coaches report that they have to spend more time managing parents than they do managing their teams (Stewart, 2006).

All coaching questionnaires and tools used to gather feedback overwhelmingly find that the number one concern for all coaches, regardless of level, is out-of-control parents (Stewart, 2006). So much so that a record number of skilled, caring, and talented coaches are leaving the profession (Pavlovic, 2009). As a veteran coach of over twenty years which consistently meant coaching hoops in the winter and softball in the spring, I always approached every season with great enthusiasm, hope, and anticipation. However, as the years have passed, I add to the list "when is a parent going to ruin it for me or my team" to the list of anticipations…expectations. I have sadly learned that it is not a question of "if" but regrettably a question of "when" will a short-sighted parent accuse me of not caring about their kid or not playing them enough? It is harder and harder, each season to dodge the "parental bombs" thrown my way. I now find myself asking, "Is this really worth all the stress that parents create?" I then remind myself how much I love coaching and how much I love mentoring young people. Maybe I should just coach orphans? Not only are parents pushing coaches out of coaching, they are burning out their own children, too (Stewart, 2006). Along the way, parents are creating a dynamic that encourages their children to question a coach's authority rather than demonstrating respect for it.

In a national survey of female athletes by Craig Stewart, Montana State University (2006), he found that even at the college level, athletes are reporting that their parents are placing too much pressure on them to excel athletically. Many reported that they contemplated stopping playing a sport they loved because of their parents. Furthermore, female athletes shared that they often felt embarrassed by their parent's unnecessary phone call or meetings with their coaches. On the contrary, however, many female athletes did report that they did, at times, feel they could question their coach's authority because their parents had also done so.

So many parents are pressuring their daughters to get their college paid for through athletics, and they will not let anyone stand in the way of that dream. Not coaches, not other families, not even their own daughter. If it is perceived that someone is interfering with the "parent's dream" that their daughter play college athletics on a scholarship, then watch out. They will take out anyone who stands in the way…including their own kid. No wonder record numbers of girls are walking away from organized athletics.

What do female athletes want? They want their parents to be spectators, not coaches, officials or players. They want other parents to watch the game, cheer and leave their teammates alone. Numerous female athletes have reported that they are horrified and embarrassed by some of the comments coming from parents (Stewart, 2006). After the game, most female athletes report that the worst part of a loss was the ride home where both they and their coach were questioned by their parents. Females athletes need time and space, just like their coaches, to reflect and unwind. They do not need to be analyzed by their parents and listen to the parent criticize their coach or officials. Female athletes should never be made to feel that their parent's love is tied to whether they played poorly or well. Certainly a coach is going to have to deal with the emotional aftermath of having a parent overly critical of their daughter's performance. And as can be seen in the research, a mess created at home will be brought to the field the very next day, as girls struggle with letting things go (Stewart, 2006).

Just like they need to be valued and encouraged by their coach, girls also need to be encouraged by their parents, too. They need to hear, "I love watching you play," or "I love watching you be part of a team; it's fun to see how well your teammates play together." When parents question their daughter's performance and then turn that into questioning their daughter's coach, it is destined to negatively impact the player-coach relationship. Rarely does that go well, in fact, usually it helps to erode the player-coach relationship, sometimes beyond repair. Sadly, that seems to be the underlying goal of some parents. If so, goal accomplished.

The impact of parents, even well-meaning parents, has greatly influenced the player-coach relationship. This appears to be a problem that is growing rather than improving. Talented, committed coaches are leaving the profession while female athletes are burning out because of the constant pressure from home to improve, play more, or get that elusive college scholarship. Playing youth and high school sports has evolved from enjoying the thrill of competition and the joy of playing with friends to seeking out that great scholarship offer. With that focus, a wedge is growing between coaches and their players. Most coaches are focused on right now and this season and how to compete successfully, whereas too many parents and their daughters are focused on where will I play next and who will give me the most financial aid. As a result, more and more girls are not fully enjoying or appreciating the moment; instead, they look beyond the present and chase the future. A coach cannot change this attitude; rather, it is up to parents to stop micromanaging their daughters' athletics and just let them play.

PART V

CHAPTER 9

Bringing It All Together
"I Just Want to Play, Coach"

> *"Worthwhile things come from hard work and careful planning.*
> *There can be no substitute."*
> ~ *John Wooden*

As a result of the passage of Title IX in 1972, female athletic participation has increased by over 500 percent. Not only are more girls participating in organized, competitive athletics, they are doing so at an earlier age (Stewart, 2001). Historically, people who coached females had a substantial background in coaching males. As a result, many of those coaches assumed that you should coach females the same way you coach males. However, now 40 years since the passing of Title IX, more and more research indicates that not only do boys and girls respond differently to coaching, they also tend to approach athletics and competition from a somewhat different perspective (Osbourne, 2002).

According to Taylor (2000), female athletes list having fun, being with friends, and enjoying competition as the primary reasons they participate in sports. Conversely, male athletes list winning and competing as their primary reasons to play. Even with passage of Title IX, eighty-one percent of all coaches working with female athletes are still male.

According to the literature, many male and female coaches approach competition differently. As a result, it stands to reason that if over eighty-one percent of all coaches of females are male, then gender issues may come into play (Kenow, 1999).

While the literature strongly supports that there is a difference between coaching males and females, it may not be politically correct to state this publically, for fear of fearing biased or worse yet…sexist. That said, there is an undeniable difference in coaching males and females and there appears to be a void for coaches seeking training, mentoring programs, or clearly developed handbooks. Coaching education programs have not kept up with the rapid advancement of female athletics at the local, high school, collegiate, or national level. There is a lack of traditional coaching resources that deal specifically with the psychological differences between coaching male and female athletes (Stewart, 2006).

As Osbourne (2002) points out, although male and female athletes share many attributes such as desire to win and enjoyment of competition, male and female athletes do have different considerations in regard to be coached effectively. As Caroline Silby (2000) reveals, coaches, whether male or female, should be aware that female athletes want to develop personal relationships with their coaches. They prefer coaches who communicate openly and are empathic. Female athletes value friendship and like to focus on team unity. They place great value on personal improvement and mastery of skills and prefer not to have their confidence challenged. With such important and documented information highlighting the difference between coaching female and male athletes, it is remarkable how few athletic programs actually offer coach's education programs or mentoring opportunities. Even fewer include detailed information and training about the differences between coaching female and male athletes.

In order to develop an in-depth, detailed and valuable training program for coaches of female athletes, several questions must be explored. First, how do female athletes respond to male and female coaches? Are there identifiable differences between male and female coaches that are gender related, or are they more style and personality related? Second, what coaching style tends to be most effective when coaching the female athlete? What type of coaching style and approach works best for the female athlete? Finally, what does the world of athletics and competition look like through the eyes of the female athlete? What feeds her inner competitive fire and sparks her desire to win?

The role of the coach in the development of the whole person is magnificent. With more and more female athletes participating at a very high level, the need to completely understand how to effectively mentor and coach them grows in importance, too.

CHAPTER 10

PHYSICAL DIFFERENCES
"DON'T DOUBT THE POWER OF MY SPIRIT
BY THE SIZE OF MY SHOE"

"To yourself and to all those dependent upon you. Keep your self-respect."
~ John Wooden

Physical differences do seem to play a significant role in the coaching of male and female athletes. While physical differences may not be the biggest difference in coaching male and females, its importance cannot be denied. While there are some obvious and important differences such as when females enter puberty and there is the onset of menstruation, most physical differences do not occur until puberty. In fact, there are little physical differences in boys and girls until puberty (Costill, 2008). According to Earle (2008), female athletes are at risk for the *Female Athlete Triad*, which can be comprised of disordered eating, osteoporosis and Amenorrhoea. Participation in sports where a specific low weight may be required can also place some women at risk for developing the *Female Athlete Triad* (Bachir, 2008).

According to Costill (2008), female athletes are six times more likely to experience knee injuries. Their smaller bone structure and extra fat mass makes their knee joints more vulnerable than males. It is of utmost importance that all coaches of girls, without exception, take time in every pre-practice and pre-game situation to adequately warm-up their female athletes. Static stretching does not work, nor is it effective. Instead, coaches of female athletes need to provide adequate time every day for a dynamic warm up that effectively prepares the entire body for competition. The medical literature without exception reports that dynamic warm-up is the single most important way to help reduce the incidence of knee injuries for all athletes. Coaches who do not take the time needed for dynamic warm-up are placing their athletes at risk and as a result are negligent in their duties as a coach, mentor, and advocate.

CHAPTER 11

PSYCHOLOGICAL DIFFERENCES
"I'M TOUGH IN MIND, BODY, AND SPIRIT"

"Just being yourself. Being at ease in any situation. Never fighting yourself."
~ John Wooden

Psychological difference is the area where most of the significant and revealing research has been completed. While there are many important similarities between the psychological profiles of male and female athletes such as desire to win, enjoyment of competition, and accomplishing team and individual goals, many significant differences do exist. For example, according to Gosselin (2002), boys generally play sports out of the individual need for competition whereas girls tend to be motivated by performing well and are much more relationship oriented. Women are more willing to try new things, particularly if it makes them perform better.

Female athletes tend to base their confidence on what others think of them rather than relying on internal sources of confidence. Women tend to need more of an ego boost whereas for men, the opposite can often be true (Wilmore, 2008). Confidence appears to be the primary factor in determining athletic success, regardless of gender. A careful

CHAPTER 12

What Motivates the Female Athlete to Participate in Athletics? "Put Me In, Coach. No Really...Put Me In"

"The journey is greater than the destination."
~ John Wooden

According to Lehmann (2003), female athletes report that they value the enjoyment of competition and making friends through participation in sports. Frequently, female athletes are attracted to sports for the elements of affiliation, skill development, personal improvement, and a social network (Sturrock, 1999). Sturrock interviewed hundreds of female athletes participating in collegiate sports and found that often, one's closest friends are teammates. Additionally, she found that athletes report that the confidence level of the team increases when teammates know each other well.

Social interaction and team dynamics seem to be features that attract females to participation in sports. While winning and the thrill of competition are important to the female athlete, more important are the relationships developed along the way. According to Sturrock (2000) girls need to have the opportunity to socialize before games and practice.

It is up to the coach to provide the unstructured, free time that athletes can have to enjoy each other's company. Team dinners, team outings and just unstructured down time can play a very important role in the cohesiveness of the team, often resulting in great success on the field or court. Coaches at all levels need to recognize that they are responsible for the social dynamics of the team. They cannot make everyone get along, and occasionally they may have to deal with a personality who is counter to the team. However, they need to provide moments of unstructured time where players can bond and connect. Sometimes the best way for a coach to master this objective is to stay out of the way and let the players coordinate and plan their social events. Coaches will find that their players are more than capable of planning fun activities for the entire team, and if the coach is fortunate, they will be invited to join in.

CHAPTER 13

Does the Gender of the Coach
Make a Difference?
"Don't Treat Me Like a Girl,
Treat Me Like an Athlete"

"Young people need role models, not critics."
~ John Wooden

Much of the literature suggests that female athletes actually prefer being coached by men. Many female athletes find male coaches more organized, skilled, and knowledgeable about the sport (Smisek, 2002). Female athletes report that they find their male coaches to be better and more organized at running practices and preparing them to compete at a high level. However, in a study by Acosta (2006), the two traits that female athletes felt most important in a coach are ability to bond and connect with players. They tend to find more in their female coaches.

Silby (2000) indicates that a specific female athlete may respond better to a male coach while another athlete my respond better to a female coach. This may be traced back to the athlete's experiences with men and women historically and may not necessarily be a reflection of the current coach. It does seem, however, that coaching style is far more significant than the gender of the coach.

Silby (2000) points out that it is not a male versus female coach issue at all. Instead it is important for coaches of both genders to understand the female sports perspective. As Mark Stevenson (2004) shares, the most important part of men coaching women is that the coach can't look at them as just women playing sports. Instead, he needs to look at them as athletes. As long as you look at them as athletes you will treat them as athletes. Steven Murray (2007) more strongly suggests that the gender of a coach should never be a factor in determining who the next coach should be. No one should ever be allowed to assume that one gender is superior to the other gender in coaching.

Regrettably, there is a growing trend in high school and collegiate athletics in making it a priority in hiring a woman for female athletic teams. What athletics administrators and the like should be focusing on is getting the best coach for the job, regardless of gender. If the best available coach is a man then the man should be hired as the next coach. The same should be true in hiring coaches for male teams. If the best coach available is a woman then she should be hired to coach the boys, no exception. However, an emerging and growing trend is to make gender-based coaching decisions rather than qualification-based coaching decisions. This is morally and practically wrong and in many ways reeks of social engineering. It didn't work with affirmative action and it will not work, long-term for the profession of coaching, but more important, for the athletes.

Many male and female athletes have been taught to devalue the athletic abilities of females and may even believe that female coaches cannot coach as well as male. Clearly, as stated time and time again, the coach's gender does not indicate how talented they are as a coach no more than the gender of a math teacher impacting how talented she is in the classroom. We are not openly hiring teachers based upon their gender. Then why are so many athletics programs making explicit gender-based hiring of their coaches? I was always taught that the athletic field or court is an extension of the classroom. While this trend is rooted in good intention, its methods in practice are all wrong. It is time to hire the best, most-qualified coach for boys and girls, regardless of gender.

Numerous studies have examined the impact of gender on the coach-athlete relationship. What has been concluded is that it is not so much the gender of the coach but much more related to their style of relating to players and teaching the skills of the game that female athletes find important (Molstad, 2007). While most female athletes report that their male coaches appear more structured and organized they also report that their male coaches are tougher on them (Frey, 2007).

While gender of the coach can play a role, particularly in the issues, social norms, and gender expectations that the coach brings into the coach-athlete relationship, far more important is the style of the coach. Female athletes want to play for a coach who respects them on and off the court, cares about them as an individual, and is a talented and skilled teacher and motivator. It does not matter if that desired coaching style is in a man or a woman. Instead, caring and talented coaches are desired by female athletes. It is erroneous to assume that all female coaches are warm and fuzzy while all male coaches are loud, obnoxious task masters.

Other critical factors besides gender that play a role in the perception of female athletes determining if this is a coach they want to play for are: athlete's age, socioeconomic status, and ethnicity. An important "X" factor that frequently goes without discussion in determining who an athlete wants to play for is playing time. Athletes who receive substantial playing time almost always report that they like playing for their coach and they have parents who like their daughter playing for this coach. Playing time is the most important factor in determining how a player feels about her coach. In general, if she plays, she has a good feeling about her coach. Of course, there are exceptions, including if the coach is verbally aggressive or abusive. Then, no amount of playing time is going to allow this athlete to feel positive about her coach.

Longitudinal studies need to be conducted that more thoroughly examine the influences that male and female coaches have with their athletes. What does seem to be very clear, however, is that a coach's gender does not appear to play a major role, rather it the coaching style that dictates and determines the coach-athlete relationship.

CHAPTER 14

THE COACH-ATHLETE RELATIONSHIP:
BUILDING TEAM CHEMISTRY
"I CARE MORE ABOUT MY TEAMMATES THAN I CARE
ABOUT YOU (BUT YOU'RE STILL IMPORTANT)"

"The main ingredient in stardom is the rest of the team."
~ John Wooden

The coach-athlete relationship plays a critical role in the development of team success and team chemistry for female athletic teams. Female athletes want to be addressed in a friendly and respectful manner and are frequently turned off by a coach who constantly yells and screams (Pendleton, 2007). According to Silby (2002), the coach of female athletes needs to be the facilitator of good chemistry. They need to build, develop, and foster an environment that encourages mutual collaboration and participation. Far too many kind-hearted, caring coaches have kept far too many players on a team in an effort to encourage the value of belonging to a team. Ironically, studies suggest that too many athletes on a team can actually hurt team unity (Pendleton, 2007).

Team chemistry appears to be a prerequisite for success for female teams, whereas for male teams, while important, team chemistry is less critical for success. Shurrock (2006) encourages coaches to help their athletes not judge one another based upon ability coupled with building the individual confidence of all of their players.

Female athletes need clear and positive feedback. Negative, unclear criticism will likely impact their confidence. As a result, their athletic performance is likely to be less productive, too. Furthermore, the coach-athlete relationship is negatively impacted which can also result in less than maximum performance.

According to Selder (2008), female athletes prefer a friendly, respect-ful atmosphere in which to train, practice, and play. They need a high level of camaraderie among players and between their coaches. They need to be involved with a team that fosters and creates a family-ori-ented team environment that effectively meets the needs of the team and each of its players. According to Demeres (2004), both coaches and athletes feel that a coach's personality is far more important than a coach's gender in determining how well a team bonds and connects.

CHAPTER 15

What Coaching Style
Do Female Athletes Prefer?
"Just Be Good to Me..."

> *"It is what you learn after you know it all that counts."*
> ~ *John Wooden*

According to Kalaska (2008), female athletes prefer a coaching style that creates a fun environment so that they can experience success and increased skill development. In order for female athletes to achieve maximum performance, they need a coach who will state their expectations upfront. All athletes, but specifically female athletes want a coach who maintains a positive demeanor and treats their players in a positive, respectful way.

Female athletes want coaches who respect their abilities and understand the different personalities within the team. Female athletes seem to respond better to coaches who spend relatively equal time and attention with members of the team in order to avoid appearing as if they have favorites (Silby, 2002). Favoritism has been shown to be a mixed bag for the team and for the athletes. For the player who is receiving the perceived favoritism, they may feel uncomfortable and awkward and may be shunned by some teammates. For the other teammates who perceive that they are not receiving enough attention, they may feel hurt or even begin to develop a negative attitude toward players, coaches, or even the team as a whole. As can be expected, this may impede any high-level success that the team may have. According to Kenow (2007), it is really important for coaches to balance their time between athletes so that they all perceive equity and fairness.

Female athletes want a coach who will not let them get down on themselves or the team. Not surprisingly, female athletes want a coach with a good sense of humor and uses encouraging words while giving honest feedback. According to Silby (2002), female athletes value a coach who challenges them in practice yet gives her space if she had a poor performance. As Dorrance (2005) points out, female athletes will let their coach know what they need and it is the coach's responsibility to be prepared and to respond.

Women want to know what they did right as well as what they did wrong. Yelling will cause the female athlete to tune out the coaches' comments, no matter how well-founded they might be. Coaches of female athletes may need to convince them that they can be successful and that they have the skills to be successful (Lehmann, 2004).

It appears that female athletes prefer a coaching style that is caring, genuine, talented, skilled, and someone who really knows the game. Female athletes want a coach who can motivate and teach them, some-one who will nurture and care about them as players and as individuals. Female athletes are looking for coaches who are immensely talented and deeply caring. They are looking for coaches who are passionate about coaching and who will help them become better people, on and off the court.

CHAPTER 16

THE ROLE OF PARENTS IN ATHLETICS
"I AM WOMAN, HEAR ME ROAR"

*"It is amazing how much can be accomplished
when we are not worried about who receives the credit."*
~ John Wooden

If you surveyed any coach at any level and asked them, "What is the most difficult and frustrating challenge facing you as a coach today?" They would almost all respond, without fail…."dealing with parents." The role of coaching and managing athletes has evolved into managing difficult, unreasonable parents. More and more parents feel as if they have a voice in organized athletics and they are not shy about sharing their unsolicited opinions. Fewer and fewer coaches feel supported by athletic director and other administrators when it comes to coaching and coaching decisions. According to Stewart (2006), parents are now so difficult to manage coupled with administrators who are providing less and less support for their coaches that coaches are spending more time managing parents and less time on skill development and program development.

According to Pavlovic (2009), a record number of talented coaches are leaving the profession due to out-of-control parents and entitled athletes. Not only are parents pushing caring, talented coaches out of coaching, they are also burning out their own children (Stewart, 2006). Many parents are creating a dynamic that encourages their children to question a coach's authority rather than demonstrating respect for it.

In Stewart's survey (2006) he found that even at the collegiate level, athletes are reporting that parent's over-involvement in their athletics is placing too much pressure on them to perform and many have seriously thought about quitting. Many athletes report that they actually left athletics because of their parent's expectation or interference with the team or coach. Many athletes share that their well-intended parents used to make car rides home from games a nightmare. If that is the case, imagine what the athlete brings back to practice the next day.

It has become too common for parents to question their child's coach in regard to playing time, position, role on the team, or tactics. As a result, more and more athletes feel as if it is acceptable for them to question the coach, too. A coach shared a story from this past basketball season of a phone call they received from a player's father. It was during the first week of the season and the varsity team had just been selected. Standard practice is for the local newspaper to do a team-by-team "players to watch" story. This father was very unhappy that his daughter was not listed in the paper as one of the "players to watch." He felt compelled to call the coach and share his frustration with the coach. He shared that his daughter was one of the best on the team and was certainly more talented than some of the girls from her team who were mentioned. He also shared that his daughter would be "crushed emotionally" when she saw that her name was not mentioned, in fact, she might quit the team. When the coach spoke with his daughter she was so embarrassed that her father contacted the coach and even shared that she didn't really care about the story. She just wanted the team as a whole to do well (LaCure, 2010).

This anecdote highlights that most athletes, specifically female athletes, want their parents to stay out of their athletic world. Instead they want them to be positive spectators for the entire team. Numerous female athletes report that they are grossly embarrassed by some of the comments from parents (Stewart, 2006).

After the game, most athletes report that the toughest part of the loss can be the ride home with their family. Female athletes need time and space to unwind and separate after a loss or poor performance. They generally do not value or even benefit from parental analysis of their performance or that of the teams. They do not enjoy hearing their parents criticize their coach or game officials. Female athletes never want to feel as if their parent's love or approval is tied to whether they played well or played poorly. Imagine the emotional mess that the coach is left to try and manage the next day at practice. As we have learned, female athletes struggle with letting things go and need to clear the air of any emotional problems or distractions. Parents need to stop being the emotional distractions…for players and for coaches.

Just like they need to feel valued and encouraged by their coach, female athletes need to feel encouraged by their parents. When the coach is blamed for their daughters' poor individual performance or for the team's performance, she is bound to bring that negativity into the player-coach relationship and that is very difficult for even the most talented coach to repair. In fact, usually this serves to destroy the relationship for now as she too has lost respect for the coach. Like her parents, she questions the coach's ability to lead the team successfully.

Midway through this past basketball season, I was greeted by an email from a parent angry that his sophomore daughter was not starting. He continued his venomous attack by sharing how talented, tough, and committed she was and continued his rant by sharing specifically on the team whom she was better than. He also included that several parents agreed with him (I can't imagine one parent who wanted his daughter to play more so that their daughter could play less), but nevertheless, he demanded to know why his daughter wasn't starting and wanted a meeting to discuss immediately. Needless to say, the meeting never occurred due to the fact that I never meet with a parent without first having a meeting with the student-athlete first. I did immediately meet with my player to see if she too had the same concerns and observations. Much to my surprise she did. She did believe that she should be starting and that she was better than many of the girls starting in front of her.

I gave her honest feedback and a true assessment of her ability and while she did have some offensive talent, her defensive skills and intensity were lacking. Ultimately, she and I never had the same positive relationship that we had always had up to that point. In fact, not only did her parents destroy my evening with their unfounded, selfish email, they destroyed their daughter's relationship with me. Her attitude, on and off the court became a distraction for her teammates and while she will have the talent to make the team as a junior, she will not. Her end of the season evaluation was filled with anger and accusations, again stating why she should be a starter and how poorly skilled I am as a coach. I have learned that the relationship with this family cannot be repaired so rather than trying, I will make a decision in the best interest of the team and not invite their daughter back next season. As long as I am the coach, gone are the days of trying to deal with unreasonable parents and selfish players. Playing a sport is a privilege, not a right and she has lost that privilege. It is my job to help my athletes learn valuable life lessons. I hope someday she will have learned hers.

The impact of parents, even well-intended parents on athletics is well documented. The problem seems to be growing rather than improving. More and more talented, caring coaches are leaving the profession while more and more female athlete's burn out from overwhelming pressure and expectations from their parents. Successfully managing out-of-control parents is an area of such critical need, that if solutions are not discovered and implemented soon, it will be harder and harder to find and keep talented coaches. According to Thompson (2009), more coaches are choosing to leave athletics coaching rather than endure the chronic abuse and unrealistic expectation of parents.

The solution is diverse and multi-layered. However, at the core is the need for athletic directors, principals and superintendents to stop being politicians and start being educators again. Far too much time is wasted by administrators who worry about how parents will react, rather than doing what is right and supporting their coaches. Until the day arrives that administrators tell unreasonable parents "No" then the problem will just continue to grow. This is not a problem that coaches can fix alone. It is up to strong, caring, and visionary administrators to stop being politicians and doing what is right for student-athletes, coaches, and teams. Administrators sadly have become part of the problem. Rather than telling unreasonable parents "No" they frequently remove the coach and hope that a fresh start will appease the parents.

PART VI

A Coaching Model Designed for Success

CHAPTER 17

BUILDING THE FOUNDATION

> *"Tomorrow, you must try once more and even harder than before."*
> *~ John Wooden*

According to Smoll and Smith (2001), coaches at all levels are hungry for coaching education and mentoring programs. Training programs that emphasize the tactical aspects of sport-specific concepts and ideas have been in existence for years. Everyone is eager to learn new ways to attack a zone defense in basketball or defend the spread offense in football, so those kinds of programs do have their merit. However, there is a tremendous void in training programs for coaches that emphasize how best to coach female athletes. While some coach's training programs do provide general "best practices," few exist that address the very specific and unique needs of the female athlete.

In a very general sense, Smoll and Smith provide some important behavioral guidelines for all coaches, regardless of gender:

•Provide reinforcement immediately after positive behaviors and reinforce efforts as much as results.

•Provide encouragement and corrective instruction immediately after mistakes. Focus on what they did well, not what they did poorly.

•Do not punish and athlete after making a mistake.

•Do not give corrective feedback in a harsh or intimidating manner.

•Use encouragement selectively so that it is meaningful.

•Encourage effort without demanding results.

•Provide technical instruction in a clear, concise manner, demonstrating how to perform the skill whenever possible.

While Smoll and Smith emphasize using a positive approach with all athletes, they do not distinguish between coaching athletes with regard to their gender. The following is a detailed, specific model for successfully coaching female athletes.

CHAPTER 18

SUCCESSFULLY COACHING FEMALE ATHLETES
ENCOURAGING INVOLVEMENT

*"Things turn out the best for those who make the best
of the way things turn out."*
~ John Wooden

Since females are attracted to sports for the elements of affiliation, skill development, developing and maintain a social network, and love for competition (Sturrock, 1999), coaches should utilize the following strategies to encourage and increase female athletic participation:

- *Encourage female involvement through friends and other social networks.*

- *Introduce athletes to a positive female athlete as a role model.*

- *Involve as many females as possible in the design of programs.*

- *Run programs so girls and women experience success and improved skill development.*

- *Create physical challenges that provide females to successfully experience their athletic abilities.*

- *Understand that some female athletes have a fear of being labeled masculine so coaches need to be sensitive to those athletes and their concerns.*

- *Allow for and encourage social interaction and development.*

- *Inform parents of team philosophy and stress that both commitment and encouragement are important and expected.*

Sometimes girls need to be encouraged to try athletics. This will mean those who coach at the youth levels are charged with the critical role of encouraging participation rather than discouraging through tryouts and cuts. It is not fair to cut a young person from a team because she does not yet appear to have the talent or skill to succeed. Young people need to be encouraged and exposed to a variety of physical activities to see if they generate an interest or ability.

CHAPTER 19

Developing an Atmosphere for Optimal Skill Building
"Teach Me, I'm Ready"

"The true athlete should have character, not be a character."
~ John Wooden

Developing optimal skill building involves both psychological and physical preparedness. Thus, it is very important for coaches to allow their players to develop and grow, both physically and mentally. Coaches need to understand that every athlete is an individual and has a unique set of conditions under which she can perform at her best (Baker, 2003). As Women's Lacrosse coach South Carolina, Kyla Heibert (2005) suggests, the coach's first words set the tone for the entire season. Here are some specific suggestions to help develop an atmosphere for optimal skill building.

• *As much as possible and realistic, involve athletes in program design.*

•*State your expectations up front. Female athletes need clarity.*

•*Explain mistakes and demonstrate correct technique. Do so in a positive and encouraging manner.*

•*Coaches need to be available and approachable if their athletes need to talk to about the sport, or something in their personal lives that may be affecting their performance or attitude.*

•*Maintain a positive attitude and treat players in a positive way.*

•*Challenge athletes mentally and physically; help them to realize what they can do.*

•*Understand and accept the limitations of your athletes.*

•*Continually use positive motivation with individual athletes and the entire team.*

•*Help athletes develop new skills. This will help them feel more confident.*

•*Coaches should avoid "watering down" sports for female athletes. Respect and encourage their abilities.*

•*Understand the different personalities of your athletes. Certain tactics that motivate some may negatively impact other members of the team.*

•*Avoid the development of cliques by mixing groups and pairing members of the team differently.*

•*Try to spend equal time and attention with athletes to avoid charges of perceived favoritism.*

•*Support athletes in their training decisions. Help them deal with pressure from parents to perform.*

•*Always demonstrate the highest level of professionalism, on and off the field. Be on time for practice and be prepared.*

•*Challenge your athletes but always be ready to listen to feedback from players.*

•*Establish the tone of work ethic at the beginning of the season.*

•*Collaborate on goal setting where the athlete, team, and coach set and reset goals together.*

It is critical that all coaches create an athletic environment that not only encourages females to participate in sports but also provides them with the tools to maximize their success. Numerous studies suggest that there are several benefits of participating in athletics outside of the ones previously discussed. For example, some studies have shown that varsity athletes have higher GPA's (grade point averages) and higher educational aspirations than those who do not participate on varsity teams (Coakly, 2006). Additionally, students who participate in athletics have better school attendance records and demonstrate stronger time management skill then students who do not participate. For these two reasons alone, the importance of athletics in a young person's life cannot be minimized or overlooked. Thus, the role of the coach as an encourager of participation in athletics for women is a powerful one of which we can never lose sight.

CHAPTER 20

Enhancing Self-Confidence, Self Esteem, and Positive Body Image
"I Am So Much More Than How I Look"

"Be more concerned with your character than with you reputation."
~ John Wooden

Although we hear athletes and coaches talk extensively about confidence, it is not an easy term to define in practical ways. Sports psychologists define self-confidence as the belief that you can successfully perform a desired behavior (Weinberg, 2003). According to Vealy (2002), there appear to be several types of self-confidence within sports, including the following:

•*Confidence about one's ability to execute physical skills.*

•*Confidence about one's ability to use psychological skills.*

•*Confidence to use one's perceptual skills.*

•*Confidence in one's level of physical fitness and readiness.*

Physical activity is one of the best ways to increase self-esteem. Sadly, many females, beginning at an early age, underestimate and undervalue their potential for competency in physical activity (Vealy, 2002). As a result, coaches can have a positive effect on women's development of self-confidence, self-esteem, and a healthy body image.

> •*Coaches should determine what sources of information they use to form pre-season or early-season expectations for athletes.*

> •*Coaches should realize that their initial assessment of an athlete's skills may be inaccurate and thus, needs to be revised continuously as the season progresses.*

A few seasons ago, I watched this unfold…firsthand. It was my first season as the girls' varsity basketball coach for Ursuline Academy in Dedham, Massachusetts. Tryouts can be tricky at best, but when a coach is new to the kids, and unaware of their skills before the tryout process, it can make for a challenging and stressful tryout experience. I was fortunate at a small private parochial school like Ursuline to have over thirty girls tryout for the varsity team; thirty girls I had never seen play before. Several underclassmen including a handful of freshmen and even an eighth grader decided to give varsity a shot.

I was struck by one particular freshman because she was almost six feet tall and seemed pretty athletic. She also seemed to not be intimidated by the competition; however, she never really separated herself either. Thus, after four rigorous days of tryouts, I decided that she seemed more ready for the junior-varsity team and could benefit from a season improving her skills. After watching her for half of the season and witnessing her move well without the ball and defending and rebound, combined with watching my team struggle with a true inside presence, I decided to invite her up to participate in a few practices. Well, she participated.

During those few practices she rebounded and defended very well, so I decided to give her some varsity game time as we were about to play a few teams that represented weaker teams on our schedule. Expecting her to perform like a nervous Frosh, she instead, scored ten points, all in the fourth quarter of her first game. Naturally, I decided to let her continue practicing with the varsity and wanted to see her get more minutes at our next game. This was against a more talented opponent than seen in her first game. Again, with extended minutes, she performed very well, and although she made some Frosh mistakes, she was also a difference maker on both ends of the court.

It was clear that she was going to stay at the varsity level. However, not only did she stay, this Frosh that I initially thought might be a strong practice player who could get a few minutes at the "five" soon became a starter. It was remarkable. I had never had junior-varsity "call up" have such an immediate impact, let alone become a meaningful starter. She defensively covered bigger and stronger girls, yet, did a great job. Not once did she seem intimidated or out-of-place. It was as if she was too young to realize how well she was doing or how talented the girl was that she was defending.

During the second half of our game against a very talented and big Fontbonne Academy team, she was asked to defend their six-two talented big who had hurt us for twelve points in the first half. This girl had already passed 1000 points for her career and was getting all kinds of looks from college recruiters. My Frosh limited her to only three points and no field goals in the second half. She reminds all coaches that we need to recognize and understand that our initial assessment of an athlete's skill or readiness may be inaccurate, and that we need to continuously assess a player's ability and talents throughout the season. I am glad I did…you will be, too.

> •During practices, coaches need to be aware of how much time each athlete spends in non-skill activities such as waiting in line or sitting off to the side while others participate.

> •Coaches need to design practices so that all athletes can develop and master skills.

> •Coaches should not let athletes get down on themselves.

> •Coaches need to allow their athletes to develop skills at their own pace. Recognize that everyone has different strengths and areas that they need to work on.

•*Coaches should use encouraging words, positive feedback, and honest, thoughtful comments.*

•*Give your athletes reasons why they have been playing a certain position and explain the reason behind the amount of playing time.*

•*Recognize that female athletes are more likely to internalize emotional issues. Yet, they do need to have you available to discuss if they choose.*

•*Build self-confidence by providing athletes with a chance to progressively master skills. This is imperative when coaching female athletes. If they do not see progress they are more likely to discontinue participation.*

•*Try to give clear, performance-based feedback. Females cannot improve unless they have clear, specific feedback.*

•*Conduct periodic individual meetings with athletes for evaluation and open discussion. Female athletes need to have feedback and they need a forum to give you feedback as well.*

•*Help your athletes set reasonable and attainable goals. Be open to adjusting them if necessary.*

•*Refrain from comments that will hurt an athlete's self-esteem. Use constructive criticism or encouragement if something needs to change.*

•*Every coach needs to recognize the effect of their comments on athletes.*

•*Every coach needs to recognize and believe that they can positively impact the self-esteem and confidence of all of their players.*

A relatively recent addition to building self-confidence literature has been research that determined how important it is that coaches are confident in their own ability to lead and guide the team. According to Feltz (2008), coaches with a higher level of coaching confidence had higher winning percentages, had players with higher levels of satisfaction, and used more praise and encouragement. Interestingly enough, Feltz (2008) also found that a coaching education program enhances self-confidence for all coaches.

Therefore, to enhance confidence, it is crucial that coaches get their team to believe in themselves as a cohesive unit, rather than to simply believe in themselves individually. Coaches need to understand that their level of self-confidence in their ability as coaches, leaders, and teachers have a direct and measurable impact on their student-athletes. Furthermore, recent research has revealed that coaches who create a climate that facilitates the growth of self-confidence and emphasizes performance improvement over winning will have more confident athletes. As a result, they generally see better results during competition (Simpson, 2006). UCLA hall-of-fame coach John Wooden never stressed winning, and instead stressed preparing to win through practice, commitment, and dedication.

Legendary coach Don Meyer never discussed winning with his players. Instead Coach Meyer believes that winning is a by-product of great preparation, dedicated athletes, and prepared and talented coaches. Wooden and Meyer are two of the finest teachers in coaching. They were confident in their abilities and as a result, their players responded to that confidence. Coaches who yell, scream, and rant demonstrate to their teams a true lack of confidence. Instead, their team watches an insecure coach, out-of-control and ill prepared to lead him or herself, let alone a team. Confidence is contagious, and it all starts with the coaching staff.

While many coaches may have an understanding of the game and may have been a successful player, many, however, lack the confidence in their ability to teach, lead, and mentor. As my high school German teacher, the late, great Joe Kroll shared every day in class, "Work daily on your weak points so that they become strengths." Confidence needs to be nurtured and groomed daily. Take the time; it is truly what separates the good coaches from the great ones.

CHAPTER 21

Body Image

"Focus on What I Can Do Rather Than What I Look Like I Can Do"

"Exercise and diet must be considered. Moderation must be practiced."
~ John Wooden

With over sixty-three percent of all female athletes developing symptoms of disordered eating between the ninth and twelfth grades (Martens, 2005), it is imperative that all coaches of female athletes understand and look out for symptoms of disordered eating. Coaches and peers play an important role in shaping attitudes and behaviors of athletes. Sadly, coaches sometimes knowingly or unknowingly place pressure on athletes to lose weight, even when they have information about safe and effective weight management strategies. In fact, in a recent study, retired gymnasts who received negative comments about their bodies from coaches or instructions about how to lose weight had significantly more disordered eating symptoms than those who did not receive those comments (De Souza, 2006). Some coaches make the decision about the need for weight control based upon appearance rather than objective, thought-out indicators.

Although all coaches must be able to recognize and effectively deal with eating disorders among female athletes in a sport setting, an even greater accomplishment would be to help prevent or at least reduce the possibility of these disorders occurring in the first place. Some of the suggestions for being proactive in reducing disordered eating in athletes are:

- *Promote proper nutritional practices.*

- *Focus on fitness, not body weight.*

- *Be sensitive to weight issues. Coaches should be made aware of the issues athletes deal with regarding weight control and diet. They should always act with sensitivity in those areas.*

- *Promote healthy management of weight. Coaches should consider their own level of fitness as they try to be a respected role-model for athletes.*

This is such a critical area of need for coaches and one that is often overlooked or ignored. It is imperative that all coaches demonstrate healthy lifestyle choices and live by example. Gone are the days of the cigarette smoking coach portrayed in the movies of the 50s and 60s. So too should be gone the days of coaches who drink to excess, yet, ask their student-athletes to make responsible decisions regarding substances.

Coaches need to eat well, exercise, and be living, breathing role models for developing a healthy, stress-free lifestyle. I am amazed at how few coaches actually practice a healthy lifestyle, let alone promote it. Coaches need to consider their level of fitness, exercise, and eating habits. Coaches should be pleased that they can promote a healthy life-style for all of their athletes in action and not just word. Look in the mirror and ask yourself, "Do I take care of myself physically, mentally and emotionally? Am I asking my student-athletes to do something that I myself do not even practice?" If the answers are no, then you need to reassess your lifestyle and seriously question the type of healthy lifestyle role model you are for young people. Coaching is a great privilege and with this privilege comes the great responsibility to be fitness and health role models for the young women we have been charged to mentor, influence, and lead. Look in the mirror.

•Do not hold team weigh-ins…ever.

•Never tease or make an insensitive remark regarding an individual's weight. Understand that weight gain is a normal and important part of puberty and adolescence for females. Your athletes already feel self-conscious about their bodies. They do not need their coach pointing out their weight gain, body size, or body changes. Instead, promote generalized fitness for the individuals and for the team.

•Allow females to have a say in their uniforms for competition. This could have an impact on their participation and may deter them from competing if they are uncomfortable wearing their uniforms. This means that all of your student-athletes should be provided a uniform that fits them comfortably. Remember, even the thin athlete has some body image concerns and will feel better about herself with a properly fitted uniform. Properly-fitting uniforms is not a suggestion, it is a necessary part of preparing girls to compete confidently and comfortably.

We have all seen the very overweight girl with a shirt that is far too tight and with shorts that are far to snug. She deserves a uniform that works with her body shape. We have also seen the very thin athlete who has her uniform hanging off of her and she spends the entire competition pulling the shoulders up because they keep sliding down. She too needs a properly fitting uniform so that she can focus on the thrill of competition rather than worrying that she will lose her top during the game.

CHAPTER 22

FOSTERING TEAM BUILDING AND TEAM DYNAMICS
"TOGETHER, WE CAN ACCOMPLISH ANYTHING"

> *"Your heart must be in your play. Stimulate others."*
> *~ John Wooden*

As we know, team members spend a lot of time together over the course of the season. Not including pre-season, camps, and summer leagues, it is not uncommon for teammates to spend three months together, six to seven days a week for two to three hours a day. It is this camaraderie that attracts many females to participate in athletics in the first place (Stevens, 2003). Team cohesion can greatly enhance the enjoyment athletes experience through participation, as well as their performance. As a result, it is important for coaches to encourage the development of positive, thoughtful team dynamics. Some important ways that coaches can foster an environment that encourages team building and team cohesion are:

- *Encouraging activities as a team outside of the sport. This will help athletes to get to know each other, which, in turn, encourages them to work together as a team.*

- *Teach athletes that it is harmful to judge a teammate's worth to the team based upon their athletic abilities.*

•*Coaches should allow some unstructured social time at the beginning of practice.*

•*Allow your athletes to have some time during practice or other training environments to laugh or feel relaxed.*

•*Recognize that team cohesion combined with talent contributes to performance.*

•*Coach's leadership style is central and essential to team building. As a coach, your ability to positively influence the team dynamics is immense.*

If you are a yeller and screamer, you will intimidate your players. Intimidated players will become cohesive against you. Obviously, that is not what you want. Allow your players the time to bond and connect, and lead by example. Stress to your team right at the beginning of the season how important you feel healthy team dynamics are to the success of the individual, but more important…how important they are to the team. Become a facilitator of team dynamics, rather than an obstacle to cohesiveness.

The more cohesive the team is, the greater the likelihood that individual members buy in and conform to team norms and expectations. Teams with higher cohesiveness better resist disruption than teams with low team unity. Teams that stay together longer tend to be more cohesive, which leads to improvements in performance. Teams with high group cohesion have fewer athletes quitting than those teams with low group cohesion. Effective coaches can help to increase the team's cohesion (Wickwire, 2003). Ineffective coaches can destroy it.

Early in my varsity coaching career, I brought my varsity girls softball team on a team trip to Cape Cod. During this extended weekend, they played in six scrimmages against other teams from around New England. More important than the playing time was the "play time." They had so much fun eating meals together, hanging out in each other's rooms and at night, doing all they could to extend curfew. I am certain if you asked any of them now, as adults, what they remembered most about the trip, no one would report that it was the games. Instead, they would all reflect on the laughter, the silliness, and the freezing cold temperatures in which they bonded, connected, and developed some life-long friendships. Take a team trip with your players at the beginning of the season. Everyone will be glad you did. I don't know if I ever coached a team more cohesive, connected, and caring about each other. We didn't have one girl develop an attitude and we didn't have one incidence of team drama. Take a team trip.

Coaches need to communicate effectively with their teams. An effective coach needs to create an environment where everyone is comfortable expressing his or her thoughts and feelings. Team building requires a climate of openness, where airing problems and matters of concern is not just considered appropriate but also encouraged (Simpson, 2006). Coaches should ensure that everyone pulls together and is committed to the group's goal.

One of the most effective ways for coaches to develop positive team dynamics when an issue does arise within the team is to hold a player-only meeting. I have found that player-only meetings are a highly effective strategy to successfully resolve any internal player tension or conflict. It can also work very well if your team has had a few poor practices in a row or has not performed well in a few games. In order to ensure that the player-only meeting works, I do lay down a few ground rules that need to be followed, without exception. First, I meet with the team collectively to go over the ground rules and instruct them what the goal(s) are for holding the player-only meeting. I then instruct them that they need to speak from a place of mutual respect and with the goal or resolving conflicts rather than creating them. Second, I share that all players must be given the opportunity to speak without interruption. Third, once everyone has been given the opportunity to speak, then teammates are allowed to ask questions or seek additional feedback. Finally, athletes are instructed that the meeting cannot conclude until they have resolved any conflict or at least come to a mutual place of understanding and respect.

A few seasons ago while coaching my varsity softball team, a few players approached me privately to share their concerns about a teammate's attitude. My first intervention was to meet with this student-athlete privately. We had a very honest and productive meeting and I left feeling like she really got it. However, a few weeks later I was again approached with the same concerns so I decided that a players-only meeting was necessary. At our next scheduled practice I instructed my team that instead of practicing today, they were going to have a players-only meeting to resolve some of the conflict and tension that had been creeping into our practices and games. My players knew how important I felt this meeting must be because they knew how much I valued practice and practice time. They knew I must be serious because I was giving up practice time to make this meeting happen. After about ninety minutes, the meeting concluded and we did some light batting practice. The energy and enthusiasm was powerful and the next day we beat a very talented team, 10-0.

Later that season, this team comprised mostly of sophomores played in the Division II Central Mass Finals for the district championship. By the end of the season, this team would have done anything for each other, whereas earlier in the season, they might have done anything to each other. This was one of the closest teams I had ever coached, and as a result of their belief in each other and their connection to one another, we overachieved and played in the finals. Make players-only meetings part of your plan for fostering team building and building team dynamics. The results will truly speak for themselves.

CHAPTER 23

BUILDING MOTIVATION

"IF YOU LEAD BY EXAMPLE, I WILL FOLLOW"

"Concentrate on your objective and be determined to reach your goal."
~ *John Wooden*

Motivation can be defined as simply the direction and intensity of one's effort (Simpson, 2006). Competitiveness is a disposition to strive for the satisfaction when making comparisons with some standard of excellence in the presence of evaluating others (Wickwire, 2003). These notions are important because it helps us understand why some athletes seem to be so motivated to achieve and others simply seem to "go along for the ride." Coaches can significantly influence the achievement motivation for female athletes and can create a climate that enhances achievement and counteracts apathy and low motivation.

All coaches must make peace with and accept that in general, they care are more motivated to succeed than their athletes. In fact, all coaches are drawn to the profession because they thrive on the thrill of preparation to succeed and are highly motivated to avoid losing. Whereas, for female athletes, while they love the thrill of competition, they generally come to athletics to make connections and develop team unity and cohesiveness.

What a strange avocation coaching really is. For most coaches, we are miserable after a loss and rarely satisfied after a win because we see the mistakes or glaring areas that still need improvement. Jeff VanGundy, while coaching the New York Knicks stated that for coaches there are two feelings: *winning and misery.* All coaches must come to accept that losing will almost always bother us more and will certainly stay with us longer than for any of our players. In some ways, for most coaches we are primarily motivated to not lose, whereas for our athletes, they hope to play well, compete, and move on to the next game. While our motivation to succeed is stronger and more apparent than for our team, there are still some valuable and effective ways to help build motivation for female athletes. We can do this by:

- *Emphasizing practice preparation and mastery of skills.*

- *Providing honest, well thought-out feedback about skill development.*

- *Allowing athletes to take responsibility for the success or lack of success of the team.*

This is a critical component for our athletes to learn. They play a very important role in the success, or lack-there-of, for the team. This helps athletes recognize that their level of preparation and motivation to prepare does impact the overall performance of the team.

I had a varsity girls' basketball team that was awful from the foul line. It cost us a few games early in the season and no matter how much we worked on free throw shooting as a team during practice, we continued to be a poor free throw shooting team. Eventually, I challenged the girls and asked them, "How many of you come to practice early or stay late to work on your free throw shooting?' Very few hands went up and as they looked around it was clear that the message had been sent and delivered. The next several practices, the majority of girls arrived early, stayed late or both, working on free throws. Not surprisingly, our team foul shooting percentage increased immediately and dramatically.

Encourage athletes to constantly consider why they participate in athletics and encourage them to reassess as needed.

- *Emphasize a "pride-in-team" approach with a unifying team goal.*

- *Ensure that coaches and teammates value each member's contribution.*

- *Place strong emphasis on good leadership from the coach and captains (discussed later in the book).*

- *Encourage unified commitment to the team effort and reward the pursuit of excellence.*

- *Use effective communication to keep all members feeling part of the team.*

CHAPTER 24

MAINTAINING FOCUS
"IF YOU CAN KEEP MY ATTENTION,
I CAN ACCOMPLISH ANYTHING"

"Be quick to spot a weakness and correct it."
~ *John Wooden*

In every sporting season, there are moments when it is difficult to maintain focus as a team. This frequently happens at the end of the season when teams are waiting for post-season play. The loss of focus can be even more dramatic if the team is not going to qualify for post-season play and they are playing out the schedule. The desire and energy to continue practicing and reviewing endless game film can wane to the point where athletes and even coaches just want it to be game night. The excitement and effort at practice begins to dissolve and players and coaches frequently report that only games at this point in the season bring the electricity. Frequently, gone is the electricity that the first week of tryouts and scrimmages provided. Rather than viewing this as a slump, coaches and athletes can use this period of time to re-evaluate goals or to develop new skills or tactics. If approached with understanding, rather than frustration, what can seem like a roadblock in a season actually becomes a positive turning point for you and the team. In the context of an individual practice, the same principle of re-evaluation can be used to redirect athletes' attention and energy where there is a lack of focus (Owens, 2001).

Athletes lose focus when practice and practice preparation becomes too routine or redundant. This can be an excellent time for coaches to "throw out" their practice plan for the day and do some fun, skill building drills that break the monotony of routine and repetition for athletes. Ultimately, if athletes are consistently losing focus, it is the coach's responsibility to reassess the work he is doing with the team and make the necessary adjustments. Some ways to do this are:

- *Challenge your athletes in practice when you believe they can meet the challenge.*

- *Enjoy each other's company when the team is together.*

- *Make practice competitive but enjoyable.*

- *Create an environment at practice so that athletes actually want to return and look forward to practice.*

- *Be prepared and allow for variety and flexibility to keep athletes interested and enjoying practices.*

- *Allow female athletes to have some feedback and input into the design of practice.*

- *Have an insatiable desire to succeed.*

- *Teach your players to bounce back from performance setbacks with increased determination to succeed.*

- *Teach your players to not be negatively affected by others' performances.*

- *Allow yourself to ease up when you sense your athletes need a break, even when it feels as if you should be pressing ahead full force.*

- *Keep yourself on track; this will help keep your athletes on track.*

- *Be in sync with your athletes in the context of practice as well as games.*

- *Be prepared and your athletes will follow.*

- *Keep your level of enthusiasm and positive energy at a peak level and your athletes will rise to that point. Positive energy is contagious.*

CHAPTER 25

CHARACTER DEVELOPMENT

"I WILL LIVE MY LIFE AS YOU LIVE YOURS"

> *"Talent is God-given; be humble. Conceit is self-given; be careful."*
> ~ *John Wooden*

Defining character and good sporting behavior is difficult. We all generally know what those terms mean, but we seldom define them accurately or agree on their exact meaning (Martens, 2006). It is getting more and more difficult with each passing season as young athletes look to professional role models who dance, point, and live it up after each basket, touchdown, or home run. While succeeding in athletics should be fun and is a cause for celebration, more and more professional athletes are demonstrating an "I" attitude rather than modeling the importance of team first. Tennis great Chris Everet, for example, says that good sportsmanship is acting in a classy, dignified way (Ross, 2005). Basketball great David Robinson defines it as playing with all of your heart and intensity, yet still showing respect for your opponents (Ross, 2005). Shileds (2000) in his book *Character Development and Physical Activity* indicated that although character and good sporting behavior are difficult to define, they fall within the general area of morality in the context of sport. That is, they have to do what is right concerning our beliefs, judgments, and actions. Far too often we see athletes, even at the high school level, taunting an opponent or behaving in ways that are not becoming to your team. Gone is the brilliance, class, and grace of Barry Sanders, who after every touchdown handed the football to the official. No dance, no mugging for the camera, just simple class. After all, Barry believed as so many great athletes before him that you should act like you have been there before. So many professional athletes celebrate when they get a first down or deflect a pass. Act like you have been there before. Be a role model and teach your athletes to behave with class and act like they have been there before. Here are some very specific strategies for coaches to help their athletes develop character:

- *You have heard it ever since you entered the coaching profession…lead by example. Demonstrate unyielding character and class and your athletes will follow suit. If they do not, they will not make it on your team. Character is contagious and it won't allow you to keep a student-athlete on your team that does not live up to the standards you live and that you demand.*

- *Never waiver on your position as a role model. You are shaping and guiding young people through life by mentoring them through athletics.*

- *Seriously consider what you do in your private life. It has been written time and time again that the ultimate definition of character is doing the right thing when no one is watching. Do you use alcohol excessively? Do you make decisions in your personal life that you would not want your athletes to make? Are you making choices that you would not want your athletes to discover?*

- *Focus on athletes' strengths rather than their weaknesses. Build their self-confidence.*

- *Don't just focus on the person as an athlete. Instead focus on the whole person and her emotional, social, and educational needs.*

- *Get to know your athletes as people first.*

- *Keep your programs' numbers small and emphasize long-term involvement.*

- *Make sure your program links with the community and neighborhood.*

A few seasons ago, my girls' varsity basketball team volunteered to work at a local Boy's and Girl's club that was sponsoring a "Breakfast with Santa." Well as you might imagine, I dressed up as Santa and my players were Santa's helpers. Watching the joy in the children's faces was powerful and watching my players give back to the community that had given them so much was inspirational. On a cold Saturday in December, for a few short hours we had become better people by giving others the gift of time. Give your community the gift, too.

•Provide your team the opportunities to volunteer to work at community food banks, or encourage them to spend time with an elderly community member.

•Have alumni return to demonstrate their post-athletic successes in life and in their personal lives.

•Have coaches you respect come and meet with your team for an hour and let your team learn from their wisdom.

A good friend of mine, Joe Minihan is one of those coaches. Joe has a powerful story. He has spoken to a number of my teams about the ability to meet and overcome challenges. He has lived those experiences. He is that experience.

Joe, a successful college athlete himself, shares a moving story about a day that changed his life forever. He was twenty-nine years old. Earlier in the day, Joe had a fairly rigorous workout involving weights and cardio. Upon completion of his workout he noticed he had a headache. Rather than listening to his body and resting, he participated in some intense pick-up hoops later in the afternoon, with the headache raging on. Shortly after playing, he collapsed. He had experienced a major stroke. At first his wife was told that he would never survive, but Joe was a fighter. He continued to respond, continued to live. Days later she was told he would never talk again, but Joe loved a great discussion so he opened his mouth. As more days passed, his wife was told, "Your husband will never walk again." But Joe, forever a stubborn athlete, wasn't going to spend the rest of his life in a wheelchair. Eventually after months of painful physical therapy, along with anger, pain, and frustration, he got out of the chair and with assistance he walked. Today, over twenty years later, he walks. He talks. He coaches and inspires young men and women that they can beat any roadblocks placed in their way. Oh sure, he walks with a measured and very specific gate. His right arm sometimes flails around like a palm tree in the wind, but he walks. I have seen him fall, literally, but he gets back up to his feet and shares with his team, "Now that's how you take a charge!" His memory is not the best so he writes everything down although he often forgets where he puts the sheet of paper.

Joe shares his story not to inspire, but to remind his athletes and all athletes to enjoy every day to the fullest. Respect your family, care about friends, and listen to your coaches...love yourself. His story serves to remind young people that life is truly a gift and one must nurture that gift. Joe's story gives all young people the healthy perspective that wins and losses, in the big picture are not that big of a deal. Your family, your friends, and your health...now that's big.

Teaching character is vital in the role of all coaches. Female athletes cannot and will not have respect for a coach that does not demonstrate character on and off the court. Female athletes want to have coaches who serve as role models. They want and need coaches who lead by example and who expect more from themselves than they do from their players.

CHAPTER 26

Helping Athletes Refrain from Drug and Alcohol Use
"Do You Walk the Walk, or Just Talk the Talk?"

> *"Tomorrow there will be more to do."*
> ~ *John Wooden*

According to Whitaker (2008), by the time young women graduate from high school, over half have tried alcohol or other substances. The concern is so great that many state athletic associations that govern high school athletics have instituted severe penalties for any student-athlete caught using any chemicals including alcohol. In Massachusetts, the MIAA (Massachusetts Interscholastic-Athletic Association) has instituted a three-tier consequence system for any students caught using drugs or alcohol. In tier one, the athlete is suspended for twenty-five percent of the competitions. Meaning if there is a twenty game schedule then the athlete will miss five games. If there is a second offense then the next tier jumps to eighty percent of the season. This can carry over to the next athletic season if necessary. Finally, if there is another infraction, the student-athlete cannot participate in any school-sponsored athletics for an entire calendar year. While there may be misguided coaches or parents who argue that the penalties are severe, it needs to be pointed out that losing an athlete for a few games is far less severe than dealing with the consequences of an athlete losing their life.

According to Whitaker (2008), alcohol related accidents are the leading cause of death among young people under the age of 21. As coaches we are charged with the emotional and physical well-being of our student-athletes. That means we must do all in our power to ensure their safety, on and off the field. For that reason, we are compelled to run our athletic programs that demand that students completely abstain from drugs and alcohol. Gone are the days where alcohol use among children was seen as a natural rite of passage. Young people do not need to use drugs and alcohol. Their very use completely undermines everything we stand for as coaches of young women, everything we try to teach them while they are under our guidance.

I am not suggesting that I always have the answers or that my way of dealing with student-athletes and drugs and alcohol use is the only successful approach. However, at the very minimum, my approach is rooted deeply in the literature, and is very honest, consistent and transparent. Every season, I hold a meeting during the first week of tryouts with parents and candidates. This meeting is mandatory for all girls who want to tryout. During this meeting, much is discussed including tryouts, responsibility, conduct, etc. However, at the core of this meeting is a clear discussion about my policy around drug and alcohol use. I share that I have a zero tolerance for any of my athletes using any chemicals at any time during the season. If they are caught using they will be removed from the team immediately, once the infraction has been confirmed. While my state athletic organization institutes a twenty-five percent loss of games penalty for the first offense, my penalty is far more severe. I have parents and student-athletes sign a contract that they acknowledge receipt of my policy and understand that it is not negotiable. While there are some coaches, parents, and even student-athletes who find this approach too severe, I counter that losing a child to an alcohol or drug-related death is the ultimate penalty. The beautiful part of my approach is that parents and student-athletes know right from the beginning where I stand in regard to children using alcohol or drugs. By signing on the dotted line, they agree to make great decisions, on and off the court with regard to substance use. Participation in school-sponsored athletics is a privilege, not a right, and to exercise this privilege my athletes will remain drug and alcohol free.

Possibly the most important component of my approach to keeping young people drug and alcohol free is my pledge to maintain the same healthy lifestyle choices that I demand from my athletes. I do not use illegal substances of any kind and my student-athletes will never see me in a bar with several empty beer bottles in front of me or partially smoked cigarettes crushed in an ashtray. How can I ask my student-athletes to make smart, healthy lifestyle choices, on and off the field, if in my private life I continue to abuse my body with chemicals? I demand nothing more from my players than I demand from myself.

So coach, take a good hard look in the mirror. Did you go out last Friday, after a big win and drink to excess? Are you smoking marijuana, in the privacy of your living room as a way to unwind? Do you still use tobacco products? In most states all of these substances are "legal" for adult usage; however, what message do you send the young women in your charge by using them? Your actions are telling your student-athletes that it is fine for me to put chemicals in my body but please don't do the same with yours. Remember, female athletes want to have coaches who serve as role-models. You cannot abuse drugs and alcohol in your private life and still be a role model for anyone.

So coach, take a good hard look in the mirror. Are you prepared to practice what you preach? Are you prepared to live a healthy lifestyle free of tobacco and other chemicals? Are you prepared to eat well, exercise, and learn how to manage stress successfully? Are you prepared to limit your alcohol intake so that it never impairs or impacts your judgment? Simply stated, "Coach, you cannot go out and get hammered on a Friday night and then step on the court the next morning feeling as if you are a positive role-model for student-athletes." If you do, then you are the consummate hypocrite and should be banned from coaching immediately. The only coach worse than a substance-using coach is one who implies that they are making great choices in their personal lives and they lie every day to their student-athletes. As awful as it is, I would rather have a coach who is honest about their substance use coaching children rather than a coach who lies and deceives. Quite frankly, neither coach has a place around student-athletes. Ultimately, there can only be one type of coach when it comes to leading by example. That is, a coach who lives a balanced, healthy lifestyle free of any substances. To date, I am proud to report that since instituting this policy over fifteen years ago, I have not had to dismiss one player for poor decision making regarding drugs and alcohol. For that matter, I have not had to attend the funeral of any of my players either. The choice is clear and certainly worth it.

CHAPTER 27

DEVELOPING TEAM LEADERSHIP AND STRONG CAPTAINS "I CAN BE A STRONG CAPTAIN IF YOU SHOW ME HOW TO LEAD"

> *"I will get ready and then, perhaps, my time will come."*
> *~ John Wooden*

Leadership can be broadly considered the behavioral process of influencing individuals and groups toward setting goals (Barrow, 1997). A leader knows where the team is going and provides the direction and resources to help it get there. Coaches who are successful leaders not only provide a vision of what to strive for but also the day-to-day structure, motivation, and support to translate vision into reality. Coaches are leaders who seek to provide each player with maximum opportunities to achieve success. Successful leaders also try to ensure that individual success helps achieve team success (Martens, 2006).

In terms of defining leadership in athletics, it has never been stated in a more clear or profound way than by David Meade, Head Lacrosse Coach for the United States Naval Academy. He said, "The essence of true leadership is making sure everyone else is taken care of before you take care of yourself (Martens, 2006). In the era of the "me first athlete,"

Coach Meade's words have never been more important. This selfless approach to leadership is at the foundation of any good captain or great coach. A skilled coach or captain who demonstrates great leadership skills will utilize the following approach:

- *Influences the growth of the team to be better citizens. Captains must not only recognize the importance of their role, they must practice it. Captains must recognize and accept that they are held to a higher standard and that they do set the tone for the rest of their teammates to follow.*

- *The goal of the captain is to improve character and life.*

- *The coach demonstrates concern with what is happening to their team.*

- *A great leader is concerned with positively impacting the future for their team and teammates.*

One of the greatest captains I ever had the good fortune to coach is named Felicia Suto. Previous to her senior year she was overwhelmingly elected co-captain by her teammates. The fact that a senior was elected co-captain was not remarkable; however, what made Felicia's election so significant is that talent-wise on a team of twelve she was number twelve on the depth chart. Felicia worked hard, led by example, and never complained about playing time. She just loved to play basketball and she loved being with her teammates. Not only was her playing time limited based upon talent, there were actually a few games where she did not play at all. However, every time I looked down the bench, there was Felicia, loud, enthusiastic, and positive. She was the consummate teammate. Not once did she ever complain. Not once did she hang her head. Not once did she confront me or any members of my coaching stuff to ask why she wasn't playing more. Let me repeat that. A senior captain, who played infrequently and at times did not play at all, never once complained about playing time, nor did she let it interfere with her enjoyment of the season. She is the role model for how all captains should lead, behave, and demonstrate selfless support of teammates.

In a coaching career that spans over twenty years, Felicia is the only captain I have ever coached who never complained about her playing time, if playing time was substantially reduced. In fact, if I had a captain whose playing time was not equivalent to a starter or significant role player, then this is how that conversation played out. "Coach, as a senior captain, it doesn't seem fair that I don't receive more playing time." My response is and will always be, "Regardless of grade in school, age, years of experience or role on the team, I always determine playing time by needs of the team at the time, coupled with skill and attitude."

Sadly, with the exception of Felicia, I have had numerous conversations with captains and other seniors who were upset about playing time and felt their desire to receive more time should take priority over the teams' needs. I had countless conversations with senior athletes over the years who felt that by being "seniors" it qualified them for more playing time. Great coaches do not play favorites and play the kids who deserve to be in at the moment, regardless of grade or role on the team. Great captains, regardless of playing time, lead by example and make sure that they always place the needs of the team first, without exception. I have had many outstanding captains over the last twenty years. Those I consider to be outstanding were always starters or at least played significant minutes. However, in the case of Felicia, she was and is, in a class by herself. She was a senior. She was an elected co-captain; and she was twelfth on the depth chart for a team comprised of twelve players. She was not a great basketball player. In fact, she was not that talented at all. I think she may have scored ten points her entire senior season. But no one worked harder in practice or in games for that matter. No one led more by example, or had a more positive attitude than Felicia. She continues to be in a class by herself and sets the standard for which I evaluate all of my future captains. I hope you have the rare honor of coaching someone like Felicia, too.

> •*A great leader has integrity, loyalty, confidence, accountability, and self-discipline.*

A great coach or talented captain demonstrates the ability to be selfless. In its purest form, they can place the needs of the team before their individual needs. The consummate captain is an athlete who even if they do not start or play substantial minutes, can still place the needs of the team first. They model selflessness and they model a spirit of "team first" in everything they do. As you might expect, this is a rare quality to find in the young people of today. Athletes have felt entitled by many overbearing, unrealistic parents.

A very successful strategy to help coaches develop outstanding leaders and dedicated captains is to have periodic, but regular meetings with coaches and captains. Female athletes, in general, will respond and rise to the occasion if they are clear about expectations. These meetings can serve to be a tremendous sounding board for both coaches and captains. If a coach reinforces what they expect from their captains then their captains will try to live up to if not exceed those expectations. Be clear with what you expect and allow your leaders and captains the opportunity to ask you why you have the expectations you do. Female athletes need to know that there are open lines of communication and they need to know that there is a forum to voice their opinions and concerns. It is your role as the coach to provide those venues.

CHAPTER 28

What Is Mental Toughness and
How Do You Foster It?
"I'm Tougher Than I Give Myself Credit for"

"Respect without fear."
~ John Wooden

Dr. David Yukelson, Coordinator of Sports Psychology at Penn State University describes mental toughness as the ability to be more consistent and better than your opponents in remaining determined, focused, confident, resilient, and in control under pressure (Jones et al, 2002). All coaches want to see these qualities develop in their athletes. Yukelson goes on to share that a key component of mental toughness is learning how to condition your mind to think confidently and be able to overcome frustration (Jones et al, 2002). As coaches we are charged with teaching our players to not allow personal frustration undermine their confidence or focus.

Journalist Chase Ruttig (2009) views athletic toughness in a non-traditional way. Ruttig describes that mentally-tough athletes are the first ones to practice, first to games, and first to get on the bus. He adds that tough athletes are team first in every way. Finally he suggests that mentally-tough players are disciplined athletes and that discipline is at the core of mental toughness (Jones, et al, 2002).

Michigan State Basketball Coach Tom Izzo always says, "Players play, but tough players win" (Bilas, 2010). Teaching our female athletes the difference between "playing" and being a "tough player" is a huge challenge for any coach at any level. As you might expect, we first need to be mentally tough in order to model that behavior for our athletes. A coach who rants and raves, and kicks and screams on the sideline demonstrates he or she is not mentally tough. Mentally weak coaches rarely instill toughness in their players. Instead, they teach their athletes to complain, question, and berate officials and even opposing players.

Duke Alumni and College Basketball Commentator for ESPN, Jay Bilias believes that mentally-tough players are alert and active. He adds that tough players communicate with teammates so they are alert and active, too. Tough players go as hard as they can for as long as they can. It is the role of the coach to teach their players that looking for the easy way out yields less than successful results during competition. As coaches we must encourage, if not demand that our student-athletes finish every drill, every sprint, and every task to maximum completion. Anything less will discourage the development of mental toughness in our athletes.

Here are some of the qualities you hope to create and inspire in the development of mentally tough athletes:

> •*Take responsibility for your actions. If you can get every athlete on your team to understand the importance of being accountable and then get them to practice it, you will have far fewer issues arise.*

> •*Look your coaches and teammates in the eye. As Jay Bilias observed, tough players never drop their heads. They always look coaches and teammates in the eye, because if they are talking, it is important to them and to you (Jones, 2010). This is really about mutual respect. Tough players are respectful and they are willing to admit when they have done something wrong. Tough players are willing to listen and willing to contemplate a new perspective other than their own. Tough players recognize the authority of their coach and respect them for their knowledge, preparedness, dedication, and commitment to the team.*

•*Tough players move on to the next play. According to Bilias (2010), tough players don't waste time celebrating a good play or lamenting a bad one. Tough players move on to the next play. They know that the most important play in any game is the next one. I remember learning that from Holliston Varsity Softball Coach, Debbie Guenther almost twenty years ago. While coaching the boys' varsity basketball team in the winter, I was asked to be the girls' JV softball coach in the spring. During the preseason meeting with all program candidates for softball, I was impressed to hear Coach Guenther share the following words of coaching wisdom. She discussed that not only was she looking for talented, skilled softball players to be part of the program but she wanted mentally tough players as well. She defined mentally tough as not lamenting a mistake but immediately moving on to the next play. She did not want to coach young women, whom after a mistake hung their heads, which in turn probably led to more mistakes. Her words made so much sense to me that all these years later I mention that I too am looking for mentally tough players who can move on from a bad play rather than dwell on it.*

•*Be hard to play against, and easy to play with. According to Bilias (2010), tough players make their teammates' jobs easier and their opponents jobs tougher. What Bilias is discussing is that tough athletes are outstanding teammates who never, in an attempt to be successful, knock a teammate or crush their confidence. Instead, tough athletes are the ones who no one wants to cover in practice or play against in a game. They give their all, all the time.*

•*Make every game important. Bilias (2010) notes that tough players do not categorize opponents and games. They know that if they are playing, it is important, regardless of opponent or time in the season. Tough players understand that if they want to play in championship games, they must treat every game as a championship game.*

•*Make getting better every day your goal. According to Jones (2002), tough athletes hate losing but are not shaken or deterred by a loss. Tough players enjoy winning but are never satisfied. As Jay Bilias (2010) so eloquently describes, for tough players, a championship, or a trophy is not a goal; it is a destination. The goal is to improve every day.*

When I was playing, the players and teammates I respected the most were not the most talented or best players. The players I respected most were the toughest players. I don't remember many of my teammates who talked more than they performed. I certainly don't remember many of my teammates who were selfish, "me first" players. But I do remember those mentally tough players who out-worked every one on the court or who out hustled everyone on the field. I was one of those players. I am now one of those coaches. Anyone can lace up the cleats but not everyone can be a mentally tough athlete. It stands to reason that mentally tough coaches will have a greater chance of developing mentally tough athletes. What kind of coach are you?

CHAPTER 29

Dealing Effectively and Successfully With Parents and Families
"My Parents Really Mean Well, Even if They Sometimes Come Across Mean"

"Patience must be strong because sometimes the road will be rough."
~ John Wooden

There is no greater issue facing coaches today than trying to effectively work with and manage difficult parents. Many parents have volunteered as a "coach" at the youth level, but have had no formal training or experience with the important fundamentals needed to be a successful coach and role model. However, even at the youth level, if they have volunteered their time, many parents can understand the challenges you face as a professional coach in trying to balance playing time with skill development and winning. Many of those parents have very realistic expectations and while they may not always agree with every coaching or tactical decision you make, they do support you and demand that their children give you respect, too. Those are the parents we all wish we had every season. If all of our parents demonstrated this style and approach, coaching really would not be that difficult. However, sadly, more and more parents are feeling entitled and feeling like they have a voice in determining how much their daughter plays or what position she plays. If they do not get their way, many parents will immediately seek out the athletic director or principal, rather than having a thoughtful conversation first with the coach.

To no coach's surprise, playing time is the number one reason for parent complaints. Every parent wants to see his or her daughter receive as much playing time as possible. In high school and college, however, the equal or balanced playing time they enjoyed in youth sports is no longer afforded. However, parents still have that expectation and as a result, complain if their daughter is not the one to see the court or field.

Parents of high school and collegiate athletes need to be educated. They need to fully understand your philosophy and what your expectations are for the season. They need to be in very clear terms to which everyone can understand and relate. Parents and players need to hear directly and in writing what the expectations are for playing time and how you as a coach make that determination. Remember, playing a school-sponsored sport is a privilege and once you have accurately and honestly presented your policy around playing time, then players and their parents can make informed decisions about whether they are fully committed to participate.

All female athletes want their parents to be spectators – not coaches, officials or players. After the game, student-athletes report that their worst experiences have been in the car ride home with their parents. Too many parents dissect at length how their daughter performed coupled with analyzing every coaching move and player personnel decision made by the coach. While many parents are well-meaning, faithful supporters of you and your program, here are some suggestions that will help avoid as many parental difficulties as possible.

- Conduct a mandatory pre-season meeting with all parents and team candidates to outline your expectations for the season. During that time you should address the following:

A.   Your philosophy as a coach. Include your background and experience that qualifies you for this position. Do not hesitate to give each parent a resume that carefully outlines your coaching background. Parents probably under-estimate your background, experience, and knowledge.

B.   Present a very clear outline of how you go about making the determination for whom will eventually make a team and what factors are involved if you have to cut an athlete.

C.   Carefully explain your philosophy about playing time. If you are a varsity coach, make sure you point out the difference between playing at the junior-varsity and the varsity level. Help players and families understand that at the junior-varsity level, playing time is guaranteed, provided the athlete attends all practices, works hard and has a team-first attitude. However, at the varsity level, since one of the key points of emphasis is on winning, playing time is not guaranteed. In fact, it is conceivable that many athletes may not play in every game or much at all during the season. They will, however, be given the chance to demonstrate their readiness for game-time every day in practice. This is a critical point to stress with the parents and you need to say it several times during your presentation. Do not miss this opportunity or move past it quickly.

D.   Make sure that you are very clear with parents and players about your specific expectations for attendance at every practice and competition. Include in that discussion the clear consequences for any unexcused absences such as family vacation, concert tickets, or a chance to skiing over the weekend.

E.   Include in your presentation a realistic and honest overview about your philosophy of no use of substances whatsoever during the season.

- During your presentation, have a very specific discussion of how to best deal with any concerns should they arise. This will help coaches facilitate open communication more effectively with parents and players.

A.   If a player has any concerns or issues, the first step is that they should ask to speak with the coach. This request should never occur in front of their teammates or immediately after a game. All attempts should be made to seek out the coach discreetly as to not draw attention to the athlete or to the coach.

B.   In almost every situation, this meeting between coach and player will resolve any of the concerns a player may have. However, if there is still no resolve, then the next appropriate step would be to have a meeting with the player and his or her parent(s). You will be best served to call for and coordinate this meeting rather than wait for a parent to suggest it. Remember, the majority of concerns expressed by your players will involve playing time. Even if they do have another concern other than playing time, this meeting between you and your player will resolve most if not all of the issues, ninety-five percent of the time. As a coach, anticipate when a player may not be feeling valued in their role and then you the coach should request some discussion time with your athlete. The majority of female athletes will appreciate you reaching out to them and it will help them to feel more valued even if it does not increase their amount of playing time. Don't hesitate to do this as often as necessary with any of your athletes.

C.   Remind parents that it is never appropriate or helpful to request a meeting with you immediately after a game, particularly a tough loss. Remind parents that after a game is when energy and emotions are running at their peak. A cooling off period of a couple of days will work wonders. Sometimes just sleeping on it is all the cooling off period that is needed. For many parents, a concern that may, at the time, appear huge and life altering, frequently decreases in importance as the days pass. Thus, agree to give them a call in a day, when clearer heads are present and offer to have a discussion with them. If the phone call doesn't resolve the concerns then encourage a meeting, face-to-face to continue the discussion. This meeting should resolve any outstanding issues.

• As a precaution, you should request that another coach from your staff join you at the meeting. If they are unavailable or you do not have an assistant then ask your athletic director to join you. This will ensure that should the meeting not go well, there is another trusted adult who can verify what was stated at the meeting.

If coaches, athletes, and players will follow these strategies for voicing concerns, all will find a mutually agreed upon resolution. Problems occur when the first attempt at a conversation is when a parent, usually immediately after the game, wants to either set up a meeting with you right away or demands to know why their daughter did not play more. There can be no worse time to have a meaningful discussion than to have it right after a game. Everyone – player, parent, and coach – deserve a "cooling off" period to develop some thoughtful and meaningful responses to their concerns. If you guide parents to wait a few days before meeting, more often than not, you can have a mutually respectful conversation that has a positive outcome. Remember, as a coach, you need to try to stay calm and try not to let emotions take over. Parents are parents and they have a very narrow perspective. They can only see the team through the eyes of their daughter and while you see the team through the eyes of the entire team, do try to take into account why they want to meet with you.

As a coach, it is very important that you are a listener first. No matter how much you may want to jump in and defend your position, make sure you give the parent or athlete ample opportunity to share their perspective. I once learned from now retired Wellesley High School Athletic Director, Ted Tripp that the key to meeting with parents is allowing them to have their say, listen, and then give them a response. He used to always say that they may not like my response but they always leave my office with a response. Please understand that you do not ever need to be verbally abused and if the parent crosses that line, respectfully end the meeting. Request that any further meetings will only take place if it involves a trusted administrator.

In order for a coach to deal effectively with parents, the coach must have effective support from their athletic director and any other administrators that oversee athletics. What many coaches are reporting is that since most parents first bring their complaints to athletic directors or other administrators, how the administrators respond is critical. To reduce the trend of problem parents and increase the support of coaches, there is only one appropriate way for administrators to respond to a parent request to have a meeting. "Did your daughter have a discussion with the coach?' If the answer is no then that parent should not be allowed to have any airtime until that meeting takes place. The second question asked should be "Did you have a conversation with the coach?" If the answer is no then the conversation should come to a close immediately. Sadly, many administrators not only take the call, they actually have a meeting with the parent without first making the athlete and parent set up a discussion with the coach. Once this type of discussion occurs the coach is now dead in the water. Once an administrator becomes the first point person they now become part of the problem. Ultimately, this coach has been so disempowered that they probably will not be able to successfully coach their team. At minimum, their relationship with the player is now beyond repair because some misguided administrator allowed a meeting to occur without first giving the coach the opportunity to address any concerns.

Dealing with difficult parents is tough enough without having misguided, poorly informed administrators cutting the coach off at the knees. I hear more and more stories of how parents are now having their first meetings with school superintendents and even school committee chairs. Bypassed is the coach, the AD, and even the building principal. If this is how your system operates, you will need to find a new system to work for because it will only be a matter of time before you are asked to find a team at another school to coach. This is the number one reason so many fine, talented, and caring coaches are leaving the profession; lack of support when dealing with out-of-control parents.

CHAPTER 30

Running Successful Practices/Developing Effective Practice Plans
"If You Are Prepared, Coach, Then So Am I"

> *"No building is better than its structural foundation."*
> *~ John Wooden*

It goes without saying that there are many coaches out there who really understand the game and relate well to their players. However, they fail to fully understand how to properly develop a highly organized and structured practice plan. In many ways, development of effective practice plans is a real art form. I think back to my very first season of professional coaching. I was the JV boys' basketball coach for my alma mater, Lincoln-Sudbury Regional High School in Sudbury, Massachusetts. My high school coach, George Horton invited me to join his staff as the junior-varsity coach. While I had no formal training, I was young, enthusiastic, and eager to learn.

He stressed to me on an almost daily basis to utilize a practice plan. However, he never really sat down with me to discuss how to successfully develop a plan. As a result, I used to just "wing it" and showed up to practice with some ideas of what I wanted to accomplish, but never had anything written down. No real thought went into designing practices from day-to-day or week-to-week. As a result, even though my team went sixteen and four during my very first season, as I reflect back, I realize that my team and players never came close to learning and mastering skills that they would have had I mastered the art of practice planning and developing successful plans.

As I assess coaches at any level the first thing I look for as I watch their practices is do they have a detailed practice plan in writing? While coaching Division III college hoops I had the opportunity to watch several Division 1 coaches conduct practices. I was amazed to find that even at that advanced level there were some coaches who did not utilize a written practice plan. Practice plans need to be utilized at every level of coaching, regardless of age or experience. We would not want teachers to just come into class and wing it so why would coaches, where the court or field is their classroom, want to come to practice unprepared?

One of the qualities that female athletes admire most in their coaches is being completely prepared and organized. Female athletes report that a coach who runs effective, organized practices instill team and individual confidence. There is no substitute for organization and preparation.

In order to run a successful practice you first need to develop a successful practice plan. A quality practice plan is the sum total and final product of your thoughts, goals and player development needs. I have found the following ideas to be very helpful when developing successful practice plans.

1.   Be very clear, as the coach what you hope to accomplish for the day.

2.   Include at the very beginning of the practice plan a section I call "important reminders." In this section you might include when the bus leaves for the next game or any changes to the game or practice schedule. You may also include some information about where you see the team headed and other important reminders.

3.   Make sure you always write the date and time that you are

practicing at the very top of the plan. It can really be helpful when you are reviewing a plan to see what date you worked on what skill.

4.   While it is acceptable to handwrite a practice plan, I have found it much more effective to type it out. It allows for neatness and more detailed organization. Plus, your players may not always be able to read your handwriting but they will be able to read anything that is neatly presented in a typed written format.

5.   Make sure that you give each player on your team a copy of the practice plan to review before practice. This not only reinforces for your players how detailed and organized you are but also gives them a written history of each and every practice so that they can review, too.

6.   In your practice plan account for every minute of time that you have for practice. For example, if you have ninety minutes of time to run practice, be sure to write down each drill and the time dedicated to it. It might look something like this:

3:30-3:40: Defensive slides and footwork drill.

3:40-3:45: Defensive stance and zig-zag drill.

7.   I have always been a fan of alternating my drills between defensive and offensive emphasis to keep the interest of players and to get them used to adjusting from defense to offense.

8.   A quality practice plan includes some indication of what players you want to see in what positions that particular practice. This is not only an effective teaching point; it also saves copious amounts of time. For example, instead of wasting time looking at who you want to play and where you want to play them, have it written down, in advance.

9.   Remember one of the number one reasons to utilize a practice plan is to maximize your time. As any coach can testify, practice time is a prized commodity and it needs to be lovingly respected and cared for.

10. Finally, at the end of the practice plan include a section of what you hope to cover the next few days of practice. Highly successful coaches are highly organized. A great coach considers what she wants to accomplish today, tomorrow, next week, and by the end of the season. Your practice plans serve to be a written record of how well you are

accomplishing your goals. They serve to be a written record for you as the coach to review when your team is not having success.

11. Take your time to develop your daily, weekly, and monthly practice plans. If your practice is at 3:00 p.m. and you start working on your practice plan at 2:45 p.m., then you are not giving your players the type of preparation they need and most importantly…deserve.

CHAPTER 31

Some Tips for Running Highly Successful Practices
"I Want to Learn as Much as You Want to Teach Me"

"Concentrate on your objective and stay the course until you reach it."
~ John Wooden

1. Never design a practice that allows athletes to just stand around. Make sure that all of your practices involve doing rather than observing. Your players master skills by doing.

2. Quickly move from drill to drill or station to station. In most situations, ten minutes is the maximum you will want to spend on any given teaching point. Any longer than that and you risk losing your player's focus. Remember, athletes today are the product of technology and they have very short attention spans.

3. Spend most of your time talking before and after practice. During actual practice time make sure that your athletes are doing.

4. Don't hesitate to shorten a scheduled practice if you are not getting the results, effort, or intensity that you desire. Better to shorten a

practice than to practice poorly.

5. Legendary Coach Don Meyer defines intensity as playing at an uncomfortable pace. Design your practices so that your athletes are challenged to grow mentally and physically every day.

6. Make your practices more difficult than any game situation. This will prepare your team for any game situation they may encounter.

7. Make your practices fun. You want athletes who are looking forward to practice rather than hoping to avoid it.

8. Stop wasting valuable time with running and sprints that do not simulate game-like conditions. I remember at a school where I was the girls' varsity coach, watching the boys' hoop coach spend over fifteen minutes at the beginning of practice running conditioning sprints. He wondered why his players had a poor practice and had nothing in their tanks. Make your athletes work as hard as possible during every skill and drill coupled with you running your mouth less and they will become finely-conditioned athletes. I am not saying that you do not need to do some conditioning on its own…you do. However, make it sport-specific conditioning.

9. Make sure you have time every pre-practice to devote to a dynamic warm-up. Far too many coaches waste time and actually place their athletes at risk by utilizing static stretching or no warm-up at all. Once your team has mastered the dynamic warm-up place your captains in charge of warm-ups and you will see results. Remember, female athletes are very susceptible to knee injuries. They need to be prepared to work hard in practice and to do this they need to be properly warmed up. You must do this every time, without exception.

10. Change it up. If you do the same drill and skills every day, your players will lose focus and their competitive edge. Challenge them daily to master a new skill or situation.

11. Use your assistant coaches. Have them participate in a drill, run drills or place them in charge of some skill set. They need to feel important, too.

12. Utilize the Whole-Part-Whole method. Briefly discuss what it is

that you are hoping to accomplish and present it as it looks in the final product. Then spend a great deal of your time breaking it down, piece-by-piece and part-by-part. Once they have mastered the parts, bring them together to master the whole. This is at the foundation of running successful practices and having your team as prepared as possible to compete.

13. Surprise your team by giving them an unscheduled day. As you start to notice that they may need a break or focus is waning, take a day off. EVERYONE will appreciate it and they come back the next day and work even harder for you.

14. Be careful about practicing too long. You want your team focused and working as hard as they can for the entire practice. If your practice is too long they will lose focus and their energy level will fade. Sometimes more is truly less. Experiment with length of time until you assess what is the most effective length of time.

15. Make sure you give your female athletes some time before practice to just hang out as a team. This is a great team builder and really helps them prepare for practice.

16. Don't be a yeller or screamer. Be an excellent communicator who calmly, yet, firmly teaches the game. If being loud and abrasive is your style you will lose your female athletes. If you know what you are doing and can teach it in a firm, humorous, and direct way, your players will respond. They might even laugh at a few of your goofy jokes. Remember to make practice fun. Your players will work hard because they respect you but they also need to laugh and smile, too.

17. Finally and possibly most important, you need to have fun, too. I love practice. I love everything about practice. Many days I am disappointed when the practice is over because I loved watching us improve; athletes mastering skills, and connecting with the players. In some ways, I enjoy practice more than games. Games are just too stressful. Whereas in practice, if it is not going well I can just blow the whistle and teach. Have fun in practice. Enjoy every minute because before you know it the season is over. Fun is purely contagious. If you are having fun, your

female athletes will have fun, too. They don't have the time or energy to try and figure out "What's wrong with coach today?" Don't be moody and don't bring your personal stress into practice. Leave the negative at the front door and truly enjoy every moment of every practice.

CHAPTER 32

Some Special Reflections

I have been blessed to coach some amazing student-athletes and some amazing teams. As I reflect back on a coaching career that now spans more than twenty years, including high school and college, football, softball, and basketball, there are some teams that really stand out. Not necessarily because of wins or accolades but because of the quality of kid I was able to coach.

I find myself really thinking about my 2012-2013 Ursuline Academy Lady Bears basketball team. This was a team that in my first season went thirteen wins, seven losses. A very solid record, but we were a team that really struggled to find our identity and soul. It seemed that I spent as much time talking with players about playing time and dealing with hurt feelings as I did helping them master team man-to-man defense. Many of my players were more concerned with their playing time than they were focused on the goals of the team. It was as if I had two sub-teams within the larger team. Most of the players wanted to win and would do anything to make that happen, and then there was the small, yet, vocal group who cared more about their playing time, even if it meant that the team would not be as successful.

We lost a tough, opening round playoff game that year. As you might expect, there were floods of tears, genuine sadness. However, once again, my girls cried for different reasons. Most cried because this loss signified the end of the season, the end of an era, while others cried because they felt cheated in their game time. They felt as if they "deserved" more playing time. I can remember looking back at the bench and watching some of the girls pouting instead of cheering on and supporting their teammates.

During the long bus ride home I knew that I would need to have off-season meetings immediately with the returning candidates to discuss the following season. I knew I had to make it very clear the expectations around attitude and factors that would be assessed to determine who made up the 2012-2013 team.

I met first with my newly-elected captains and listened. I listened to their observations, their perceptions. I heard, really heard what they had to say. They too noticed that some players only cared about themselves and didn't care as much about the team, or the team's success. My two newly-elected captains were deeply committed to making sure that the 2012-2013 season was not only a great season as defined by wins but that all members of the team would be on the same page. This would be a "team first" team. And it was.

What a true pleasure the 2012-2013 Ursuline Academy team was to coach. Right from the beginning of tryouts I could tell that the off-season talks with captains and returning players had worked. We were becoming a basketball family. We trusted each other and the players had each other's back. Starters, when they came out of the game, cheered loudly for the players who had just subbed in for them. It was beautiful to watch, even more beautiful to experience. Girls understood and more importantly, accepted their roles. They knew the expectations to be a member of this team. They had to be "team first," always. In some gentle way, this mandatory "team first" expectation allowed this team to bond, connect, and eliminated the pressure to see your name in the stat sheets. You just needed to be "team first," always.

This team was deep, talented, and we had some athletes. We could hit the three pointers and we could pound it inside. We really were a complete team. On our way to a seventeen and three season we scored at an incredibly high pace and were very stingy on defense. We could score quickly and in bunches; at times, we would extend a two-point lead into twenty within a matter of a few minutes. The girls bought in and they had each other's backs. It was about the team and they were doing things that had never happened before at the school.

During the first round of the state tournament we drew a tough team out of Wareham. They had a couple of girls who could flat out score, but they were not deep. We were. As we prepared for them we knew that we could run them out of the gym if we got contributions out of all our players. We were very athletic, deep, and we wanted to run and push tempo. We did. Early in the season I realized that in order for all of my players to truly feel that they were all important members of the team, they needed to receive some game time, every game. And they did. The state tournament was no different. All twelve of my girls saw the court, and we won by almost thirty. It was truly a team win. It was the first playoff win in many years for the program and it was amazingly satisfying to watch the team, parents, and fans celebrate "team first."

Next up in the South Sectional Quarter Finals was a defensively tough Old Rochester team. They were only giving up thirty-five points per game and played at a very slow, methodical pace. They were, in fact, the polar opposite to my team. We wanted to run and play at a very fast pace for thirty-two minutes. Old Rochester wanted to keep the game in the thirties and make us work for every basket.

We had a great week of practice and had them well scouted. We joked that we knew them better than they knew themselves. For some reason, the game was moved to a Saturday, 1:00 start. No one wants to play a game on a Saturday at 1:00, let alone a tournament game. As the game progressed, both teams played as if it were a 1:00 game on a Saturday: sloppy play, poor shooting, but what a great defensive slugfest.

We managed to take a five-point lead after the first quarter; however, we continued to miss important scoring chances. With just over a minute left in the first half we were up by seven and really had the momentum. Neither team could score, but Old Rochester really struggled to put it in the ocean. However, as all coaches know, it only takes a moment for momentum to swing and the momentum was about to swing in a very deep and meaningful way. With just over thirty seconds to go in the half we stole the ball in the backcourt and were fouled, hard, going in for the lay-up. One of our best foul shooters was on the line and she gave us a chance to go up by nine going into the locker room for half time. The first one rimmed out. She looked like she had just lost the Olympic Gold. The pressure of a big-time tournament game was all over her face and she didn't wear it well. She missed the next free throw; ball didn't even make it to the rim. With just over fifteen seconds remaining until half time, Old Rochester inbounded the ball against our trapping, full-court defense and brought the ball to the deep corner. With time for only one ball reversal, the Old Rochester player skipped the ball, over the top of the defense and found her teammate, in the corner. With one of my players closing out on her nicely, she launched a three from the left baseline corner. Nothing but net and the buzzer sounded. We are up by four, yet a five-point swing had just happened; Old Rochester grabbed the momentum.

The second half was a back and forth, emotional drain that found neither team taking more than a three-point lead. With just over forty seconds to go in the game, we found ourselves down by two. Two points seemed like ten because points were so difficult to come by. Down thirty-five to thirty-three, and having missed our last six foul shot attempts, I called a timeout. I mentioned that while we had done a great job getting the ball inside to our big, we had not been efficient at finishing or hitting our free throws when fouled. Thus, I decided to first look for an open three and while we were not shooting well from behind the arc either, we had all season long. As expected, Old Rochester extended their match-up zone and we could not find an open look for the three. We did, however, find Morgan O'Donnell, our six-foot sophomore center, inside, with a girl on her back with fifteen seconds left. She caught a great bounce pass entry feed from the wing and made a power move to her right getting fouled on the way up. There were twenty-two priceless seconds on the game clock. I never told anyone this, not even my assistant coaches, but when Morgan was fouled I didn't think she had a shot at making the free throws. She was only sixty percent from the line during the season and was two for ten during this game.

However, with the class, grace, and poise of a veteran beyond her years, she calmly hit both foul shots. The game was tied at thirty-five and looked destined for overtime. But destiny is a funny thing and sometimes she changes her mind, without warning, and she was changing her mind. We just didn't know it yet. We would have to wait twenty more seconds to find out what she had in store for us.

Old Rochester called their final time out and my bench mobbed Morgan with such joy and enthusiasm; it had to be our day. We discussed our defensive alignments and personnel coverage. I reinforced that we could not foul, or give up any second shots. I shared that if we got the rebound or steal, we had to take the ball, hard, to the rim for victory. We came out in man and we forced the action to left. As the clocked slowly tick down, one painful second at a time, my starting two guard, Courtney Sepe almost came up with the play of the game. As she rotated on defense, she nearly stole the ball for an uncontested, game winning layup. Instead, destiny was not our friend, at least at that moment and her right foot had stepped out of bounds of the sideline steal. Old Rochester maintained possession and with seven seconds left, inbounded the ball from half-court. We denied every pass, and doubled off the ball. Yet, just before a five second count could be called, Old Rochester's point guard came off a screen and grabbed the inbound pass. She took three dribbles and heaved a shot from about twenty-five feet. I had a great angle. Too good actually and I watched the flight of the ball: perfect arc, nice rotation, and right on target. As the buzzer sounded to end the game and force overtime, the ball fell gently threw the net. Ball game. I stood in absolute disbelief. It was surreal and certainly could not be happening. Not here, not now, not to my girls. The basketball family. Old Rochester celebrated; their fans stormed the court, meanwhile, my girls, every one of them, collapsed on the court. It couldn't be. Their season couldn't be over, but it was.

I had to shake hands and congratulate the Old Rochester coach. He had designed a great defensive game plan and his girls executed it. They kept the game in the thirties and they hit the big shot. They had played their style and they won. I walked out on to the court, hugging my players, helping them into the locker room. As I entered the locker room it was as if I was attending a funeral. The air was heavy and thick with sadness and disappointment. It was overwhelming. I joined my girls in the team room and tried to talk, but I couldn't, I was starting to cry and no words left my mouth. I had to walk away to try and collect myself, not that I did not want my girls to see me cry, but I was ready for a major cry. They needed me and I needed to collect myself. I couldn't. Several times I came back to the team room, only to walk away again to try and get my voice back. I knew what I wanted to say, I just could get the words out.

Finally, after several attempts, I rejoined my team, my basketball family. Through the tears I told them how proud I was of them and how much I loved them. I told them that we didn't lose today, we ran out of time. I shared how amazing it was that both halves ended with a buzzer beater. As I reflected on an incredible season, the best regular season in school history, it was painfully clear that not only did we lose the game, but we were losing the seniors. Their last memory of playing basketball would always be a buzzer beater to knock them out of the state tournament. Their final memories of high school basketball would be the overwhelming emotion, tears, sadness, and love. They had overcome so much and became a family. Today, they grieved as a family and it was truly beautiful to experience. To watch people who cared so much about each other, give to each other was truly a gift. I hope all coached get to experience the "gift." No I don't want you to lose a big game at the buzzer. Actually, I do not want to ever experience that again either. Wow, that is tough. But I do want you to experience the "gift." The gift of being important in a young person's life. The gift of knowing that you have been blessed to coach so many fine student-athletes. The gift of recognizing that it is a true honor to lead a sports team. At the end of the day it goes well beyond the X's and O's, it's about the role modeling, the mentoring, the laughter, and yes, even the pain and disappointment. You are a coach. You are a gift.

CHAPTER 33

GRAFTON

Finally, I reflect back on to the 2013-2014 season; my first season with the Lady Indians of Grafton High School. I remember when I first applied for the position, I knew that Grafton had not had much success over the years with its girls' basketball team. However, it was not until I walked into the gym for the first time that I saw just how little success Grafton had over the years in girls' basketball. The gym was beautiful: great hard wood floors, clean, and full size. This would be a great place to teach the game. However, as my attention was called above by the myriad of banners, neatly hanging from the rafters I noticed that the girls' basketball banner was blank. No league titles…ever. Now I really wanted this job. There was only one place to go for Grafton girls' basketball.

I was called back for a second interview. This time I would be meeting with the Athletic Director and the three captains. The captains asked me the standard questions; however, when I asked them some questions, it was their responses that made me think, *I really want this job.* They shared with me that they wanted a coach who would teach them how to play and how to get better. They wanted a coach who would believe in them and would make playing the game fun. They didn't know it at the time, but they were describing me and I knew this would be a great match.

Even though I have coached for over twenty years, I was still blown away by their description of their previous coach. They shared that when they lost a game, which they did seventeen times the previous season, the coach would yell, scream, and then the next day make them run. Not basketball running, but punishment running. No wonder this team continued to lose; their coach ripped apart their confidence and refused to teach them how to play the game. Instead, she focused on punishing rather than building, belittling rather than motivating. It was clear after meeting the captains that they were looking for me and I was looking for them. Student-athletes who wanted to improve, have fun, compete, and work hard doing it. It was a great match.

The previous three years before I had arrived, the seniors on my team went four and sixteen as freshmen, three and seventeen as sophomores, and three and seventeen as juniors. I promised my seniors, my entire team that if they bought in, worked hard, and were team first players, we would have success. We might even make the state tournament. I remember how crazy they thought I was. They looked at me almost as if to say, "Where did this guy come from? Doesn't he know we haven't had a winning season in years?" I did know; however, I could assess talent and effort and while we were frightfully short, we were athletic, quick, and had some talent. They just didn't know it yet. We were going to compete but I had to teach them how to play man-to-man defense, how to successfully run a motion offense, and how to shoot.

As coaches we really are teachers and that is what draws us to athletics. We love teaching. We love practice and we love teaching. I was a teacher again. I was teaching my girls how to play fundamental basketball and teaching them how to believe in themselves. They bought in and we went eight and twelve that season, barely missing qualifying for the state tournament. As coaches we work harder when our team is less talented than we do if our team is very talented. For the true coach, the coach who is in this profession for the right reasons, you thrive on building a program. You love watching your teams "get it." You revel in the success that you helped create. You hate when the season is over, yet, you begin preparations for the next season the very next day. For you there is no "off-season." You are a role model, mentor, and leader year round, 365 days a year. You may do more to ensure a successful season in the off-season than you do during the season. Stay in touch with your players in the off-season. Watch them compete in other sports. Celebrate their successes.

At Grafton, we celebrated. Not a winning record or qualifying for the state tournament, but instead we celebrated getting better, gaining confidence, becoming a team, and yes, becoming a family. Watch for us next season. We will have a winning record and we will qualify for the state tournament. All firsts since 2004. Who knows, one day we might even put our name on some banners.

CHAPTER 34

G.O. and Savvy

As coaches, sometimes we are blessed with a special player. They may not be the most talented or athletically gifted, but they bring a level of leadership and competitive spirit that instantly makes the entire team better. As I reflect on a coaching career that has seen almost 500 career wins between softball and basketball, I find myself reminiscing about those special players.

I have been blessed to have coached many talented players, some who had the team-first mindset that was truly a pleasure to be around. But I decided to go deeper into the memory banks to pull out some of my all-time favorite team-first players. The type of student-athlete that you proudly built the foundation of your team around. The type of student-athlete who you knew represented your team, your school and your community with class, grace and dignity. I did not have to delve to deep to find those types of players: G.O. and Savvy.

G.O. was not the tallest, the fastest or even the most athletic kid on any team. However, she loved to participate in sports. As a nine year old she was the only girl on her Pop Warner football team, in fact, in most games, she was the only girl on the field. She played offensive line and I sense that she enjoyed hitting boys…hard who questioned why she was on the field. Who knew that this nine year old was building the foundation of leadership on the football field that she would take with her to the basketball court well into high school.

As a basketball player it was always abundantly clear that she was not the best athlete on the court, but no one ever outworked her and I don't know if I met a basketball player, male or female with a greater basketball I.Q. Maybe it was because she was from a basketball family. Her two older brothers played up through college and she was dragged from gym to gym to gym. Or maybe it was because her father was a basketball coach and he dragged her from gym to gym to gym. I sense her "basketball family" played an important role in her developing a true love for the game, but like so many other female athletes G.O. developed her own independent love for competition and love of being with teammates.

What I loved about this kid every time I had the chance to watch her play is that she talked and pointed on defense. And even though her varsity coach told her not to shoot, she celebrated each basket with the joy it deserved. As a 9th grader as a member of her freshman team she was given the MVP award by her coach at the banquet. Not because she led the team in scoring but because she led the team. It was clear she was a natural born leader and she was destined to lead her teammates. At the end of her junior year of basketball she was elected to Team-Captain by her team.

As a senior she started every game. She did not lead the team in scoring or assists, not even in the top five; but she was an excellent defender and led the team in rebounds. Most importantly…she led the team in encouragement, leadership and was a profound example of how to live your life, on and off the court. An honor roll student, she volunteered in the community, was active in her church and was a tremendous ambassador for her team in the classroom and in the community.

In the games that I was privileged to see, I was impressed by how much she truly enjoyed playing. It was gratifying to see a young person thrive on the essence of participating in high school athletics…participating. I found myself envious and I wished she was on my team. We could have used a few more team-first players who brought a level of dedication and commitment rarely seen in this generation of millennials.

G.O. was a member of a very successful team and during her senior year they managed to win their league and win their first two tournament games. I had the good fortune of attending her Central Massachusetts tournament game held at Clark University. What a great game. Both teams came to play and to play hard. Neither team was ever able to extend the lead by more than five.

G.O. played and played a lot of minutes, she defended well and continued to be a rebounding machine. Down by two with less than a minute left in the game, her coach called a timeout to discuss the situation and provide instruction. I heard her say to her team: "Don't worry guys, we got this!" Well as coaches we all know the valuable and at times, hard lesson athletics teaches us. Tonight was not their night and her team lost by four.

I watched as she walked off the court as the buzzer sounded and could see that she looked almost stunned. But then the harsh reality of the game, her season and her career immediately set in. She cried. A cry from a very deep and meaningful place, the kind you hate to watch and even more you hate to standby and do nothing. It wasn't just because they had lost the game, but because she had lost her basketball. Basketball had been part of her life, all of her life. She played youth, AAU, summer leagues, travel and high school. In middle school she was the score keeper for the varsity team. Basketball wasn't something this kid did, basketball was part of this kid; and because a buzzer sounded, that was over.

For just a few moments, I hated coaching and I hated athletics. Why should someone feel that kind of pain after a game? However, I quickly came to my senses and realized that she would overcome her sadness and replace it with the memories of joy, of teams and of basketball. G.O. was a walking billboard for the place that athletics has in the development of our young people. She was a shining star of why participating in athletics is great for girls and creates the next generation of women as leaders and mentors.

Savvy is G.O's younger sister, younger by just a year. Savvy loved to participate in sports too, although she never found the passion for softball and football that her sister did. However, Savvy played basketball and like her sister, she meant business every time she stepped on the court. If Savvy had the ball stolen from her she would sprint down the court and steal it back. She played hard, she played tough, and she played with a chip on her shoulder. Always with class, but she made it clear that while she was on the court the opponent was just that…the opponent. I am not sure she ever truly enjoyed winning but it was clear she did not enjoy losing. It was that spirit that made her a good teammate. She had high expectations of herself and expected at least as much from her teammates.

Like so many female athletes, Savvy spoke her mind. She wasn't shy about sharing her opinion and frequently wanted to know the rationale behind a particular coaching decision or offensive or defensive philosophy. As an observer, she seemed to drive her coaches crazy, so much athletic talent coupled with so much sass. She was never disrespectful but she reminded her coaches that respect was truly a two-way street between coach and student-athlete. Savvy served to be an example of how all coaches need to interact with their female athletes. Female athletes need to have an environment that fosters leadership and independence coupled with the opportunity to be an individual and a coach that nurtures respect rather than demanding it.

As a younger player in travel basketball, Savvy was one of the few athletes that I had ever seen who truly relished playing defense and always asked if she could be the "designated doubler?" I remember many times wishing I had someone like that on my varsity team that brought a defensive toughness and respect for the game. If you were a teammate of Savvy's you had better play defense…or else. Savvy reminds us as coaches that all aspects of a sport are important and should be taught as such.

I remember watching Savvy's final high school basketball game. It was the first round of the state tournament. A solid team but they had lost some key members to graduation the season before. I watched her work hard, as usual, on defense. She played with such confidence, the kind of confidence that only being a senior can bring. You could see that some of her younger teammates were shying away from the spotlight that only tournament ball brings. I was most impressed on her will to compete, quite frankly, her will to win. She would not let any of her teammates give less than maximum effort.

This spirit, this leadership caused her team, including the "young guns" to play an excellent second half. However, as with all athletic events, there would be a loser and tonight Savvy's team was on the losing end. She didn't cry, she wanted too, but there were too many people around. Instead she congratulated her teammates and her coaches. She was saving those tears for another time, another venue…when she was ready to share them with the world.

A few weeks later at her basketball banquet she was asked to speak on behalf of her team by her coaches. She was articulate, animated and funny. She was Savvy. Now was the time, now was the right time for her to share her tears; not with strangers for all to see but with her teammates, coaches and families. She concluded her speech by reflecting on her team, her coaches and her family. It was her reflections of her family that allowed her to grieve and share her grief.

She reminded us as coaches that our players all have families and their families are vitally important to them. Savvy reminded us as coaches that maybe the reason we have the good fortune to coach special players is because many of our players have special families. Families who recognize team-first, support athletic participation and care about the entire team not just their kid. I had sensed that Savvy's family got it, and as a result, she did too.

Savvy enjoyed playing, she knew it was a game, and in the big picture she kept a healthy perspective. It wasn't all about trophies and banners, it was about having fun. She wasn't solving world peace or finding the cure for cancer, she was playing a game; and when playing a game you are supposed to have fun. Just don't ever steal the ball from her…!

As coaches we must always remember this too. We are privileged to coach and mentor, teach and support. This is a game, always has been and always will be. We as coaches impact whether our student-athletes have fun, love coming to practice and love playing in the game. We can make it fun or we can make work. Our players have plenty of time to work, make it competitive, make it fun and let them take your life-lessons you taught them. Who knows, you might just be mentoring the next great coach?

I hope, in a small but significant way I have mentored my own daughters, Savvy and G.O. to be the next great coaches. They have made me a better coach.

CHAPTER 35

SOME FINAL THOUGHTS

Coaching female athletes is a wonderful and exciting way to spend a career. Just the other day, one of my junior softball players asked, "Coach, how do you deal with coaching high school girls? How do you deal with all the drama?"

I smiled and responded, "For every situation where there is drama or disappointment, there is a moment where I can sit back and watch you and your teammates celebrate a victory, or I think about all of the great relationships I have developed over the years. Those moments, those relationships…this makes it all worthwhile!"

Anyone who has had the privilege of coaching female athletes understands how awesome it is watching them gain confidence, master skills, and play the game out of pure love of participation and the thrill of competition. In many ways, their motivation to play is the same motivation we have to coach. We love competition and we love the endless hours of preparation. Most important, however, is we love our players.

As coaches of female athletes, we are charged with not only making them better athletically, but also making them better people. All athletes want to know that their coach cares about them beyond the athletic field. However, female athletes need to know that not only does the coach know what he or she is doing; he or she also cares about the athletes as people, too.

Use *Hormones, Hair Elastics, and a Helmet* as a guide to successfully coach female athletes. Recognize that your coaching style is more important than all the "X's and O's" you could ever design. Remember, you set the tone for your athletes. Your players want you to value them as people, not just as athletes. They want you to care and they want you to make them better athletes, but they also want you to make them better people. They want you to teach them the game, but they also want you to teach them life lessons. There can be no greater purpose.

My greatest joy, second only to being called "Dad," is being called "Coach." It is my calling in life and strongest professional passion. We have been blessed to carry a whistle and to be a critical and key influence in the lives of young people. While winning is important, developing winners in life is the number one goal. You are a coach and you mentor and touch lives. Wow, we have been truly blessed with the gift. Honor and respect the gift. As Coach John Wooden shared, "When we are out of sympathy for the young, then our work in the world is complete."

REFERENCES

Acosta, V.R. (2000). Women in intercollegiate sports: A longitudinal study: twenty-three year Update, 1977-2000. Women in Sport and Physical Activity Journal, 9(2), 14-19.

Baker, J., (2003). Coach behaviors and athlete satisfaction in team and individual sports. International Journal of Sports Psychology, 34, 226-239.

Becker, A., (2005). Expectancy information and coach effectiveness in intercollegiate basketball. The Sports Psychologist, 19, 251-266.

Burke, K.L., (2005). The effects of coaches' use of humor on female volleyball players' evaluation of their coaches. Journal of Sports Behavior, 18, 83-90.

Carpenter, L.J., (2001). Back to the future: Reform with a woman's voice. Academe, 23-27.

Carron, A.V., (2002). Compatibility in the coach-athlete dyad. Research Quarterly, 48, 671-679.

Chase, M., (2007). Do coaches' confidence expectations for their team predict team performance? The Sports Psychologists, 11, 8-23.

Croce, P., (2006). How different are the sexes? In Coaching Soccer, ed. Tim Schum. National Soccer Coaches Association of America. NTC/ Contemporary Books, Chicago, Illinois, p. 322-323.

DeWitt, J., (2001). Coaching Girls Soccer, Random House Inc., New York, NY. 15-23.

Dorrance, A., (2006). Training Soccer Champions, JTC Sports, Raleigh, NC. 2-45.

Felder, D., (2000). Role conflict, coaching burnout, and the reduction in the number of female interscholastic coaches. The Physical Educator, 47, 7-13.

Frankl, D., (2008). Gender bias: A study of high school track and field athletes' Perceptions of hypothetical male and female head coaches. Journal of Sports Behavior, 21, 396-407.

Freeman, W. H., (2001). Physical Education and Sport. Boston: Allyn and Bacon.

Garcia, C., (2000). Gender differences in young children's interactions when learning fundamental motor skills, Research Quarterly for Exercise and Sport, 65, 213-225.

Glesne, C., (1999). Becoming Qualitative Researchers, New York: Addison Longman.

Grisaffee, C., (2001). The effects of head and assistant coaches' use of humor on collegiate soccer players' evaluation of their coaches. Journal of Sports Behavior, 23, 57-67.

Kenow, L.J., (2002). Relationship between anxiety, self-confidence, and the evaluation of coaching behaviors. The Sports Psychologist, 6, 344-357.

Kenow, L.J., (2005). Coach-athlete compatibility and athlete's perception of coaching Behaviors. Journal of Sport Behavior, 22, 251-259.

Kimmel, M.S., (2000). The Gendered Society, Oxford University Press, New York, NY.

Lirgg, C. D., (2004). Influence of gender of coach on perceptions of basketball and coaching self-efficacy and aspirations of high school female basketball players. Women, Sport, and Physical Activity Journal, 3, 1-14.

Lott, B., (2007). Women's Lives: Themes and Variations in Gender Learning, Brooks/Cole, Monterey, CA.

Martens, R., (2004). Successful Coaching (3rd ed.) Champaign, IL. Human Kinetics.

Maslin, H. L., (2008). Men coaching women, Coach and Athletic Director, 68, 16.

Medwechuk, N., (2004). Effects of gender bias on the evaluation of male and female swim coaches'. Perceptual and Motor Skills, 78, 163-169.

Molstad, S., (1997). Perceptions of female basketball players regarding coaching qualities of males and females. Journal of Applied Research in coaching and Athletics, 2, 57-71.

Moritz, S.E., (1996). What are confident athletes visualizing? An examination of image content. The sports Psychologist, 10, 171-179.

Morris, T., (2004). Self-confidence in sport and exercise. Sport Psychology: Theory Application and Issues, 2, 175-209.

Osborne, B., (2002). Coaching the female athlete. Psychological Foundations of Sport, 428-437.

Parkhouse, B.L., (2006). Differential effects of sex and status on evaluation of coaching ability. Research Quarterly for Exercise and Sport, 57,53-59.

Pastore, D.L., (2002). Two-year college coaches of women's teams: Gender differences in coaching career selections. Journal of Sports Management, 6, 176-190.

Pipher, M., 1994. Reviving Ophelia: Saving the Selves of Adolescent Girls, Ballentine Books, New York, NY.

Sabock, R. J., (2001). Should coaches be gendered? Coaching Review, 10, 28-29.

Silby, C., (2000). Games Girls Play: Understanding and Guiding Female Athletes, St. Martin's Press, New York, NY.

Simmons, C.D., (2007). The effects of gender on the psychosocial development of college female student-athletes. Research Quarterly for Exercise and Sport, 59, 7-12.

Smisek, J., (2006). Coach the Athlete, No the Gender, Coaching Soccer, 4, 319-327.

Stewart, C., (2000). Why female athletes quit: Implications for coach education. Physical Educator, 57, 170-186.

Vealy, R., (2001). Understanding and enhancing self-confidence in athletes. Handbook Of Sport Psychology, 2, 43-82.

Weinberg, R.S., (2003). Psychological foundations in sport and exercise. Champaign, IL. Human Kinetics.

Whitaker, G., (2005). Male coach/female coach: A theoretical analysis of the female sport experience. Journal of Sport and Social Issues, 9, 14-25.

Whitaker, G., (2008). Role modeling and female athletes. Sex Roles, 18, 555-566.

Wrisberg, C.A., (2006). Quality of life for male and female athletes. Quest, 48, 392-408.

ABOUT THE AUTHOR

Photography by Dharmendra Acharya
www.dharmendraacharya.com

Dr. Jeff LaCure, Psy.D, M.S.W., LICSW is a sports psychologist, clinician, psychology professor, and successful high school and collegiate coach with almost 500 career wins as a basketball, football, and softball coach. He is the author of several books including *Adopted Like Me, Remembering: Reflections Of Growing Up Adopted, Raising Our Children's Children, Room In The Heart,* and co-author of *A Father's Advice with Love* with Mike Tougias (Author of *The Finest Hours,* made into a successful Disney movie). In 2018, Dr. LaCure will be releasing *The Lifelong Search for Oz.*

Dr. LaCure is currently on the Graduate Psychology faculty for Cambridge College. He maintains a successful private counseling practice in Grafton, Massachusetts and is the founder and director of the LaCure Basketball Academy. Dr. Jeff LaCure is an active member of the Massachusetts Basketball Coaches Association and a member of the MIAA Partners In Prevention. He is called on nationally to provide coaching clinics for high school and collegiate programs and provides leadership training to athletes at the youth, high school, and collegiate levels. Dr. LaCure is the father of four children, all who, to no one's surprise, participate in athletics.

Learn more by visiting www.drjefflacure.com